GUITAR

A book for every kind of guitar player
– for the beginner, or for the more
expert . . .

– for the jazz guitarist, for the
Spanish-style soloist, or for the three
chord strummer . . .

NEW REVISED EDITION

Guitar

Dan Morgan

CORGI BOOKS

GUITAR

A CORGI BOOK 0 552 99183 X

First publication in Great Britain

PRINTING HISTORY
Corgi edition published 1965
Corgi edition reprinted 1965
Corgi edition reprinted 1966
Corgi edition reprinted 1967
Corgi revised edition published 1971
Corgi edition reprinted 1971
Corgi edition reprinted 1972
Corgi edition reprinted 1973
Corgi revised edition published 1974
Corgi edition reprinted 1975
Corgi edition reprinted 1977
Corgi edition reprinted 1980
Corgi edition reprinted 1981
Corgi revised edition reissued 1985

This book is set in 11/12 pt. Century

Corgi Books are published by Transworld Publishers
Ltd., Century House, 61-63 Uxbridge Road, Ealing,
London W5 5SA, in Australia by Transworld
Publishers (Aust.) Pty. Ltd., 26 Harley Crescent,
Condell Park, NSW 2200, and in New Zealand by
Transworld Publishers (N.Z.) Ltd., Cnr. Moselle and
Waipareira Avenues. Henderson, Auckland.
Printed in West Germany by
Mohndruck Graphische Betriebe GmbH, Gütersloh

Contents

Guitar

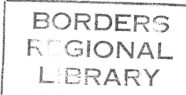
THE GUITAR TODAY

When the first edition of this book was written an old friend of mine who was also a writer and a guitarist shook his head and said: 'You're too late! The guitar boom is on its way out. By the time that book gets into the shops nobody will want to know.' That was over twenty years ago, and I'm happy to say that dear old John couldn't have been more wrong. We've progressed from the Swinging Sixties into the Troubled Eighties and GUITAR, both the instrument and the book, are alive and well.

My own involvement with the guitar has never been greater. I play more guitar and listen to more guitar than I ever did. AND MORE IMPORTANT, I get more pleasure from the instrument than ever. It seems to me that there is a kind of snowball effect here. The more you know about the guitar, the more you want to know, and the more enjoyable the experience becomes. This week you find that you can play quite easily passages that would have been too difficult a few months ago. With that kind of achievement under your belt you are able to look at new difficulties confident that in a week, a month, or perhaps even a year, they too will be mastered.

During the past few weeks I have been to a Jazz club and listened to the incredible playing of Fapy Lafertin, the Belgian gipsy, who sounds like a re-incarnation of Django Reinhardt. I have attended a meeting of the local Guitar Society and listened to Alexander Mac-Donald's Aranjuez Trio playing a concert of Spanish music by Albeniz and others. Through the medium of television I have listened to Diz Disley, another Reinhardt disciple, talking about his experiences as a musician and playing. I have also had the pleasure of

1

hearing once again the incomparable Joe Pass playing both as a solo artist and in company with Oscar Peterson.

In a more active role I have played several Jazz sessions with my own quartet of Spanish Guitar, Plectrum Guitar, Bass Guitar and Drums. At other times I have discussed the instrument with fellow players and picked up one of my guitars at any spare moment during the day for a practice or recreational session of varying length.

I'm not trying to impress you with my energy, but merely pointing out that for anybody who is interested in the guitar in any of its forms there are opportunities today that just didn't exist twenty years ago. Even the smallest town now has its guitar teacher, often even its own guitar maker like my friend Nick Penny, who has acted as doctor on many occasions to my own instruments when they have needed attention.

I have spoken elsewhere in this book about my own early days with the guitar, and the isolation I felt at the time, playing what was then a comparatively unknown and strange instrument. There's no question of isolation now, the aficionadoes of the guitar form a vast club with a variety of interests ranging from Heavy Rock to Bach and all kinds of variations in between.

Some people keep to their own particular favourite style to the exclusion of all others, whereas others move quite happily from one type of playing to another and enjoy them all.

My own sympathy is with the latter type of player, because I believe that there is enjoyment to be gained and technical points to be learned from the playing of all types of music. Learned is a key word here, by the way. I am not ashamed to say that I am still learning about the guitar, indeed I hope that it will always be so. In this I am in good company, because Segovia himself has said: 'I was both my pupil and teacher, and I am learning still. It is better to be a pupil of an art at 90 than a master at 14.'

At the present time I have four guitars, each of which plays an important role in my musical life. For Plectrum style Jazz playing I use a vintage Gretch Chet Atkins model which gives me the sound I like to hear. But more and more since its acquisition I find myself playing

Jazz finger style on a Takamine nylon strung cutaway, which is basically a Classical guitar with a built-in pickup. Playing with the quartet mentioned above I find that the natural guitar sound of this instrument contrasts well with that of my colleague Don's Ibanez Steel strung Semi Acoustic Electric, which he plays mainly with a plectrum.

For Classical playing I have the nylon strung Spanish guitar built for me by my friend Jorge (Ken Gooding), a beautiful instrument that has matured over the years so that its tone now compares in my opinion with that of a Ramirez. And last, an old Harmony Sovereign acoustic guitar which I can and do play anywhere on my travels from here to the South of Spain.

The guitar in one of its forms is seldom far from my thoughts or hands. After over forty years of playing the instrument I still find something new and interesting about it every day. This experience enables me to say in all sincerity that the guitar is the most rewarding of instruments to play, offering an infinite variety of sounds and pleasures for those who are willing to spend some effort in exploring its possibilities.

If you are at the beginning of that exciting road I envy you. This book will help you along the way as its earlier editions have so many others in the past. I have received letters from as far away as India and Australia from players who began with it and found it useful, and that in itself is a great reward for my efforts.

If you are a newcomer, begin at the beginning and take your time. If you are already a guitarist of some accomplishment you may want to skip the second section, which could be too simple for you. The last thing I wish to do is insult your intelligence. But whatever your standard of playing, I hope you will find something of interest in the rest and some suggestions that may help broaden your guitaristic horizons.

Chapter One

BUT YOU CAN LEARN . . .

Not so many years ago, when TV was still science fiction, there used to be a piece of furniture in most front rooms known as a piano. Mum polished it with loving care, and occasionally somebody in the family would open up the lid and actually *play* it. Certainly, everybody who was anybody had a piano – and everybody's son or daughter from about the age of eight upwards was given a shiny brown music case and packed off to Miss Crotchet's for lessons once a week.

Most kids hated it, of course. What red blooded boy wants to sit practising scales when the rest of the gang are out playing cricket, or football? And girls have important things to do too, I suppose. It's not surprising that very few of these pressed pupils ever became brilliant pianists. Out of all the people I knew at school who learned, or rather, went for lessons, I can think of only one who is still playing a musical instrument – and he is a saxophonist.

I was lucky. My parents didn't have a piano. So, despite the fact that it was the done thing, there was even less point than usual in *my* having lessons. As a result of this I reached the age of fourteen before the bit of music there was in me began to look about for some way of expressing itself . . . and discovered the guitar.

Today that doesn't sound at all an unlikely choice, but at the time I'm talking about the average person didn't know a guitar from a banjo, or that thing George Formby played. The guitar, I felt, was for me. I spent hours looking in the music-shop window, worshipping its shape, and I spent the rest of my time with an ear glued to the radio, listening for the slightest hint of a guitar-like sound. I just knew that when I got my hands on a guitar it would sing magically beneath my fingers,

4

reproducing my musical dreams.

The infatuation was so strong that I managed to save up enough for a deposit, and ordered my first guitar from a magnificent mail order catalogue. This too, was something of an adventure. In those days HP was a very naughty word with respectable business people. You paid cash, if you had it – or even owed for years and years – but instalments were very non-U.

When the guitar arrived it was a black, cello-built monstrosity with a neck so warped that the strings nearly cut your fingers off when you tried to play anywhere past the third fret. I was delighted. At last I had a real musical instrument, a guitar of my very own, with shining new steel strings – no case, that would have been *too* expensive. After all. the guitar cost £3 15s.

One thing spoiled my complete happiness. I ignored it at first, as one would a blemish on the cheek of a loved one, but eventually I was forced to recognize its existence. My guitar might look all right, but there was clearly something wrong with it, because I couldn't *play* it. The strumming of the untuned strings began to pall after a time, and beyond that there seemed to be nothing. The guitar was quite incapable of reproducing those tunes that were in my head.

About this time I remembered my friends with their shiny music cases and with a sinking feeling I began to make some deductions. Could it be that even something that looked as simple as guitar playing had to be learned? perhaps even to the extent of having – I choked on the thought – *lessons*? And if you had lessons – who gave them? The guitar didn't come into Miss Crotchet's category of respectable musical instruments, alongside the violin and piano – and it wasn't even on the semi-respectable fringe, with such oddities as flute and clarinet.

After a great deal of vain enquiry I was forced into the recognition that I was on my own. If I was going to play the guitar, I would have to teach myself. *So I did* – which is just about as true as saying 'They lived happily ever after.' Life isn't that simple. My troubles had just began. I went along to a music shop and bought a tutor, expending another hard-saved five bob. It didn't take me long to find out that the tutor was useless. It just didn't contain what I was looking for. All I wanted was a concise statement – say a couple of sentences – that would tell me *how to play the guitar*. Once that was settled, *I* could get on with it.

This was a very frustrating period in my young life. I was now four pounds to the bad, and no nearer to playing the guitar. The black monster stared at me in mute reproach. Rather than admit defeat, I went along to the music shop again and bought *another* tutor. And found it as useless as the first one. A suspicion began to grow in my mind that perhaps the fault was not after all in the tutors – written by well-known, and no doubt highly respectable musicians – but in *myself*. Five bobs notwithstanding, it seemed that the golden key to guitar playing was not handed out indiscriminately to everybody who applied. The only thing I could do to preserve my investment and whatever measure of self respect I had left, was to start practising the exercises in the tutors.

So it began, the clicks and buzzes, the sore fingers, the boredom . . . Only the thought that soon, when I had proved my worthiness, the golden key would be handed to me, kept me going. *I'm still waiting* – or rather I would be, if I hadn't realized along the way that there just isn't any golden key, or magic word, which once given will enable you to play the guitar. There are a number of tutors on the market which promise to teach you to play in a few hours, a day, or a week. Each time I see one of them I feel a twinge of the old frustration. Such claims are complete nonsense, as the people who make them are well aware. It takes time to play the guitar, and it takes work.

Just how much time and how much work? Well, that's up to you. How far do you want to go? If all you want to do is play simple song accompaniments, you're obviously going to get where you want to be a lot quicker than somebody who wants to be a solo guitarist. For one thing, you don't need to read music, and for another, you needn't bother about practising scales. In other words, the two most forbidding obstacles to a beginner can be eliminated right away.

What you do have to learn – and this applies to anybody who wants to do *anything at all* on the guitar – is to play CHORDS and to understand the CHORD SYMBOL system. For this reason I have devoted the second section of this book to the study of chords and their use in accompaniment playing. The key word here is USE. A lot of boring, theoretical work will not be necessary, because as soon as you've learned only two chords, you can start right in playing song accompaniments that will sound musical enough to whet your appetite for more.

By the time you have worked your way through Section Two, accompaniments will no longer present any problem to you. As you go along you will build up your repertoire of chords in different keys, and there will be song accompaniments for you to play, educating your fingers in the use of those chords. This may take you as far as you had originally intended to go, but I'll be very surprised if you aren't so hooked on the guitar by then that you want to go on and explore the tremendous possibilities of the instrument. If you do feel that way, you'll find plenty of food for thought in the remaining two sections.

Clearly, it isn't possible to set down everything there is to know about every type of guitar playing in one book, but in Section Three you will find special notes and musical examples of the most important styles, combined with quite a bit of general information that will be useful to you. Section Four is the *working section*, placed where it is, so that you can take it or leave it. In this section you will find all the basic information you need to start you on the road to *real guitar playing*. But don't try to go too far, too quickly, or you may be disappointed. You can't become a Segovia or a Django Reinhardt overnight.

It's amazing how far you can get unaided, if you have the right kind of applied pig-headedness. I have never had any kind of musical tuition, much less in guitar playing, but that hasn't stopped me holding down professional jobs in groups playing everything from light orchestral music to modern jazz. Perhaps my proudest moment as a self-made musician was when I was asked by the Local Education Authority if I would run their classes in guitar playing.

I began my first lesson with the flat statement: 'No one can teach you how to play the guitar.' This brought a sudden hush to a room which only a moment before had been a madhouse of chatter, tuning noises and assorted party pieces. So far, so good, but it also happens to be true. No one *can* teach you how to play the guitar – *but they can help you to learn.* There is a subtle difference here that is all-important. If you are going to play the guitar, then *you* are the one who is going to do the work. I found this out the hard way, so you can take my word for it. You'll get out of the guitar what you put into it.

Anybody with the normal number of fingers and average intelligence *can* learn. Like riding a bicycle or using a typewriter, playing the guitar is a skill which can be developed by practice. Once you've learned the basics laid down in this book, the only limitations are the extent of your will to work and your innate musical ability.

This book is dedicated to the lone student who is trying to fumble his way towards playing the guitar, fighting against discouragement and frustration, and wondering if he will *ever* be able to play like the people he hears on records, TV and radio. If you have a teacher, you're lucky – if not, it is my hope that this book, derived from my experience as a guitarist and teacher, will make the hard road a little easier, and save you taking too many wrong turnings.

Am I making guitar playing sound too difficult? I hope not. That is not my intention. You *can* teach yourself to play. Django Reinhardt, Wes Montgomery, Johnny Smith and Ivor Mairants, to name but a few, are all self-taught players . . . and all great guitarists. Even Andres Segovia has said: 'I have been my pupil and teacher.' Different styles, different temperaments, these artists have one thing in common – love of the guitar . . . the sound of the instrument, the holding of it and the actual playing.

A couple of years ago I had a touch of madness and decided to buy myself a really good guitar. I went along to Ivor Mairants and we spent a morning going through most of his large stock, trying one instrument after another. It was a long process; made even longer by Ivor's method of testing. Not for him the brief run over the fingerboard and a few tentative chords. Each time he picked up a guitar he would not put it down again until he had played a complete piece on it. This was no exhibitionist pose, but an expression of his genuine love for the sound and feel of the instrument. Each guitar, once in his hands, demanded the respect and dedication of his undivided attention.

The only good reason for your wanting to play the guitar is that you feel the same way. It's no flight of fancy to say that the measure of your love will dictate just how good a guitarist you are to become. This – if anything – is the golden key to guitar playing.

Chapter Two

YOUR GUITAR

There are two basic types of guitar. The first has metal strings, the second (normally called the Spanish guitar) nylon strings. Even at this early stage it is important that you should understand the essential differences between the two types, because if you don't you could waste a lot of time and money.

The best Spanish guitar ever made would be completely useless to someone whose ambition is to play in a beat group, and the most fabulously ornate Electric guitar with three pickups, tremolo arm and on board pre-amp would be equally unsuitable for someone who wants to play Classical Finger Style.

So where do you start? Well, unless you have your heart set from the very beginning on becoming a Classical Finger Style player, I would recommend that you begin by purchasing a reasonably priced acoustic steel strung instrument. The tuning and left-hand fingering of metal and nylon strung guitars are identical, so you have nothing to lose by following this course.

You can work through Sections Two and Four of this book on a metal strung instrument, training the fingers of your Left hand and learning the notes on the fingerboard. If you later decide that you would like to go on to the Finger Style nylon strung guitar nothing you have learned will be wasted.

But before we go any further I must give you one very important warning! Whatever you do, NEVER put metal strings onto a guitar which was built to carry nylon strings. Spanish guitars are much lighter built than metal strung guitars and the higher tension needed to tune metal strings can cause irreparable damage.

This may be obvious to you, and you're probably wondering why I lay so much stress on the matter. But I will always remember with a shudder of horror the time when a lady turned up at one of my classes with a beautiful little French made finger style guitar, ornate with mother of pearl inlays and over a hundred years old. (The guitar – not the lady!) Full of good intentions she had taken it along to a supposedly reputable music shop on the previous day and asked them to fit it with a new set of strings. This they did – metal ones, under the strain of which the neck of the guitar was already warping visibly!

To help you avoid this kind of pitfall, please study the illustrations and descriptions of the different kinds of guitars on the following pages carefully.

Metal strung guitars can be divided into three types: the Acoustic, the Acoustic/Electric or Semi-Acoustic and the Solid Electric.

THE STEEL STRUNG ACOUSTIC GUITAR
The Round Hole Acoustic Guitar, sometimes known as the 'Jumbo' or 'Dreadnaught' is the most suitable type of instrument for a beginner from several points of

10

view. It is very similar in appearance to the traditional Spanish guitar, but more heavily built to withstand the extra tension of steel strings. Another important point is that the fingerboard of a steel strung guitar is usually narrower and slightly curved, making it easier to play in some respects than a Spanish guitar, particularly when dealing with moving chordal passages.

This instrument has no pickup or means of amplification and depends solely on the strings and the resonant properties of its own body for the sound it produces. It is used by a large number of Folk, Blues and Ragtime players, both as a solo instrument and as an accompaniment to the voice. Because of its limited volume it is not suitable for playing the solo lead in a group, but it is a very useful instrument on which to learn the basics of guitar playing.

THE SEMI ACOUSTIC GUITAR
This is the instrument mostly favoured by Jazz players. Generally speaking it has a slim body which produces less un-amplified sound than the Dreadnaught. This limitation is not important however, because it is fitted with pickups which convert the vibrations of its steel strings into electro magnetic impulses which are then fed into an amplifier. Thus the major part of the sound comes from the speaker of the amplifier rather

than the instrument itself and can be adjusted to make it louder or softer by a simple movement of a volume control knob.

Normally played with a plectrum the Semi Acoustic guitar is used for both comping (accompaniment playing) and single note soloing in Jazz groups. Of late years there has also been a growing trend among Jazz soloists to play the Semi Acoustic with the fingers of the right hand, a style which increases the self-contained qualities of the instrument and converts it into what has been described as a Lap Piano. The leading exponent in this field is without doubt Joe Pass, whose recordings will be of interest. This is a fascinating style, but it would be only fair to make it clear at this point that it is also a difficult one to play because it requires a greater knowledge of the fingerboard and the principles of Harmony than possibly any other style. I shall explain more about this subject in later chapters.

THE SOLID ELECTRIC GUITAR

This is the instrument that is seen in a vast variety of forms in Rock and Pop groups, and could in that sense be classed as the most popular guitar. The Solid is fitted with pickups like those on the Semi Acoustic, but as it consists of little more than a block of wood with a guitar neck attached it depends entirely on an amplifier for the production of sound. For this reason a beginner buying a Solid must be prepared at the same time to go to the expense of buying an amplifier, which could cost him as much or even more than the guitar itself. This being so, I would not happily recommend a complete beginner to start off with a Solid.

Later on, well that's a different matter, because when it comes to group playing a Solid has several advantages. Firstly it is usually quite light in weight, which is a consideration if you are playing in a standing position all night with it hanging from your neck. Secondly, the action of a solid can be made very light, which makes it easy to play, because there are no structural acoustic properties to consider in the making of the body. The shape of a Solid guitar is limited only by the imagination of the maker, as will be seen from illustration C.

The third point about Solid guitars is that because there is no need of any consideration of acoustics in their construction a Solid can be made quite cheaply. This is not to say that you cannot pay a very high price for a Solid electric guitar with special electronic refinements and gimmicks, but there are a number of very reasonably priced copies of the original Les Paul model around that are quite adequate. Just bear in mind that without the help of an amplifier your Solid will produce nothing more inspiring than a tiny 'Plink' – in contrast with an Acoustic, which you can play anywhere and produce a musical sound.

THE TWELVE STRING GUITAR

This is mainly a vocal accompaniment instrument, long used by Folk artists like Leadbelly (Huddie Leadbetter). It has a characteristic, jangly sound of its own which you may or may not find attractive. The sources of this different sound are the twelve strings, which are grouped in pairs, as on a Mandolin, the bottom four pairs tuned in octaves with one thick and one thin string side by side. This means that what would sound as a single note on a normal guitar is automatically doubled up on the twelve string instrument

The intervals of the tuning are the same as for the standard 6 string guitar, so that the normal fingering for scales and chord shapes can be used. However, the pitch is normally four semitones lower, which means that the usual fingering for an E Major chord produces as C Major sound. For this reason the tuning given below is known as the C tuning.

C TUNING FOR 12 STRING GUITAR

1st pair	C (Unison)
2nd pair	G (Unison)
3rd pair	Eb (Octave apart)
4th pair	Bb (Octave apart)
5th pair	F (Octave apart)
6th pair	C (Octave apart)

As mentioned above, the 12 string guitar is most useful as a vocal accompaniment instrument, but it is not one which I would recommend to a beginner. For one thing its twelve strings and their intervals make it a difficult instrument to tune and if anything sounds worse than a 6 string guitar out of tune it is a 12 string! Apart from that, the different naming of the chord shapes can easily lead to confusion.

THE SPANISH GUITAR

Finally we come to the true, classical guitar, the instrument of Segovia, Julian Bream and John Williarms. More lightly built, its nylon strings give it a warm, sensitive tone of quite a different quality from that of the metal strung instruments. A good Spanish guitar is responsive to the touch of the fingers to a degree not found in a steel strung instrument and tone production becomes much less mechanical and more intimate. For one thing, the thicker, more pliable nylon strings with their lower tension feel quite different under the fingers of both the Left and Right hands.

More than any of the other guitars, the Spanish guitar is a complete instrument, full of rich possibilities for any musician who is willing to work and study to develop those possibilities. I'm not trying to put you off learning to play the Spanish guitar, but I think you

should understand from the outset that this most rewarding of guitars is also the most demanding. It is not an instrument for the dilletante or casual strummer.

BUYING A GUITAR

It follows from what has been said above that the most sensible type of guitar for a beginner to buy is a reasonably priced steel strung acoustic model similar to that shown in Illustration A. The tone of such an instrument can be surprisingly good and satisfying, especially if you have never had the pleasure of making your own music before.

If you'd like to hear the acoustic guitar at its ultimate, listen to the recordings made by Django Reinhardt with the Hot Club de France in the thirties, many of which are now available on re-recorded LPs. This may sound a rather prehistoric kind of reference, but in my opinion and that of many other guitarists, those performances have never been equalled since.

You should be able to pick up a reasonable second hand acoustic guitar for around £25, which is pretty cheap for the amount of pleasure it can give you.

If you're really stuck on the idea of an Electric, a Solid will probably cost you £40 or £50, and then there's the amplifier to think about, so you're going to be committed to around £100 before you start. But do read the chapter on Electric Guitar in Section Three of this book before buying. A Semi Acoustic would cost you rather more, say £70 or £80 for the instrument, and here again you would probably want to buy an amplifier as well.

You should be able to buy a reasonable second hand Spanish guitar for about the same price as an Acoustic. Cheap Spanish guitars used to be known as Valencianas, after the city where so many of them were made, but today they are just as likely to be Japanese – and none the worse for that, I hasten to say. Admittedly it is rather above the Valenciana class, but my own Takamine is a delight to play and beautifully made.

TONE

Don't buy a guitar solely on its appearance. You may be tempted by some beautiful looking instrument only to find that it makes a sound like a leaky bucket. Sound is what you are looking for.

Your guitar should have a round, full tone in the bass and a singing, sustained sound on the top strings. Some guitars, because of bad construction, will sound flat and woody, with a muffled tone even on the open strings. Others will be over-balanced on the bass side, with nothing in the treble but a tinny tinkle.

Draw your plectrum or the fleshy part of your thumb across the strings mid-way between the bridge and the end of the fingerboard. Does the sound ring on for some time after the stroke, or does it die almost immediately? If it fades too quickly try another - try another in any case, because it will give you some basis for comparison.

The chances are that the guitar will be out of tune, so ask the dealer to put it in tune for you before trying it. If he doesn't know how, he hasn't any business selling guitars. After all, would you buy a car from a salesman who didn't know how to drive?

If you try several instruments you will find a surprising difference in their tonal quality and sustaining power. And these differences may not always bear any apparent relationship to price. Sometimes, because of the strange vagaries of the guitar maker's craft, which is more of an art than a science, a cheap guitar may have a better tone than a more expensive one.

I stress the matter of tone particularly because it is of prime importance, but you must also remember that tone is to some extent a subjective matter and people have different opinions. What you should be looking for is a sound that pleases you, personally.

Within the obvious limitations of your pocket your instrument should give you the best possible value for your money. By the way - if you have a friend who is already a player, do your best to persuade him to go along with you and help in this testing. For one thing, he will already be aware of many of the points raised here, and for another you will be able to listen to him playing the guitars and get a truer impression of their qualities.

ACTION AND TUNING

Assuming that the guitar you are trying is tuned to concert pitch - and this is essential, because only at this pitch will the strings possess the correct tension -

now is the time to check on Action and Tuning. Find the 12th fret by counting upwards along the neck on the 1st string. Unless the guitar you are trying is a Spanish guitar there should be a position dot, or dots at this fret to guide you. When you have found it, press the 1st string down onto the fingerboard just behind the fret and hit the string with your Right thumb or plectrum.

Then take your Left hand finger off and play the open string. The two notes should form a perfect Octave. If they don't, either the bridge of the instrument is out of position, or the Action is too high.

Action is the word used in describing the amount of force needed to press the strings down behind the frets. Thus we speak of a high or a low Action, according to the height of the strings above the fingerboard. It will be obvious to you that the higher they are initially, the more effort is needed to press them down firmly behind the frets.

Generally speaking the strings should not be more than a quarter of an inch away from the fingerboard at the 12th fret, and they are in some cases quite a bit nearer than that. Just how near they can be is a complicated formula referring to bridge height, neck pitch and fingerboard straightness understood only by alchemists like my guitarrero friends Nick and Ken. As a mere player I take these mysteries on trust and leave them to the experts.

At the beginning your fingertips are sure to be soft, and when they start to get sore (as they will!) you're going to think that a quarter of an inch Action at the 12th fret is pretty high. The only certain consolation I can offer here is that the soreness will wear off in time, if you keep on playing, because your finger ends will grow their own protective coating. I stress the phrase keep on playing because at one stage I didn't touch a guitar for over a year, and when I came back to it I found that although I hadn't quite forgotten how to play, I had to go through the uncomfortable business of toughening up my finger ends all over again.

Most Semi Acoustics have an adjustable bridge, so that you can make some change in the action yourself, but on a flat top acoustic the action you buy it with is the one you are stuck with, apart from calling in the attention

18

of an expert (and even he may not be able to cure the trouble if it is too bad). That being the case, my sincere advice is that if the action seems rather high give the instrument a miss. Trying to play on a high Action at this stage could be a serious discouragement from which you might never recover.

Put at its simplest, the ideal Action could be defined as one which is low enough to make fingering easy, but not so low that the strings foul the frets and produce unpleasant rattles.

When the first edition of this book appeared I played it safe by suggesting that for a really superb action the experienced player usually bought one of the American made guitars like a Gibson, a Guild or a Gretch. Whilst all three of these are still fine instruments, their present day prices are too high to make them a practical proposition for the average amateur or even semi-pro player. Fortunately, due to commercial demand, there are a number of other makes now on the market that offer very good value at un-fancy prices, such as Ibanez, Washburn, Takamine, Ovation and Yamaha. Unless you're prepared to take out a second mortgage to buy one of the three G's all of these makes are worth looking at and trying when you get to the stage of wanting something better than your second-hand Acoustic.

Beyond all talk of brands, the main criterion is to find an instrument that suits you personally, that gives you the sound you want and that you can play comfortably. And remember, as with any other specialized purchase, go to an expert. If you buy from a reputable instrument dealer, you'll get what you pay for in the matter of quality, and you'll get a bonus in good advice.

Chapter Three

FIRST THINGS

Now that you have the guitar, the very first thing to learn is *how to tune it*. This may sound crashingly obvious, but I have met students who have been messing about with the instrument on their own for months and are still totally incapable of tuning it. I even had the bloke, who when I complained of his lack of tuning, said: 'But I paid twenty quid for this guitar, and they said it was in tune when I bought it!' – and he wasn't kidding.

A plectrum guitar should hold its basic tuning pretty well, once its strings have had time to settle down. But even so, the tuning should be checked *at least* each time you pick it up to play. During a playing session an experienced guitarist checks his tuning constantly and adjusts as necessary. In solo playing, the fact that a string is out of tune shows itself immediately to the ear when playing a passage across the strings. In chord playing, an out of tune string will make the chord sound wrong, and two out of tune strings will give a total effect something like musical toothache.

One method of tuning is to use a piano. The illustration below shows you where to find the notes you need for this.

It is helpful when tuning to a piano to place your foot on the right-hand pedal. This will cause the piano note to sustain and make it easier to compare the corresponding note on your guitar. Begin by finding the E above Middle C – then pick your 1st string. Remember, the 1st string is the *thinnest* one on the instrument, and the

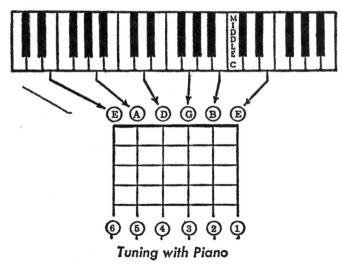

Tuning with Piano

6th is the *thickest*. I stress this point, because students often find the numbering of the strings confusing in the first stages.

Well, how is your 1st string? Chances are it's out of tune. If you're starting from scratch with a new set of strings, or a guitar that hasn't been tuned in years, then it will be way out. To make matters worse, it is likely that you will have some difficulty in comparing the pitch of the piano note with that of the guitar. The reason for this lies in the different tones of the instrument, coupled with the fact that at this stage your ear is not accustomed to such exacting tasks.

Don't worry too much if you're a bit of a 'tin ear' at the outset. I have known students who held up the class for long enough during the initial tuning sessions, winding away grim faced at their creaking machine heads. Tuning was about as simple to them as boarding a moving bus with a parcel under each arm and they usually ended up sharp or flat, leaving the final adjustment to me. And yet, later on, some of these same students have become exceptional players, with great left-hand agility – and tuning, as their ears have developed, presents no difficulty at all.

Now – is your 1st string sharp (higher) or flat (lower) compared with the piano note? Chances are that it's flat, but to make sure, try the nearby notes on the piano, going down one by one until you find the note that does correspond with the sound your 1st string is making. When you've found this note, begin to tighten the string gradually, checking as you go along, until it comes up to pitch.

When you're satisfied that the 1st string is in tune, find the note B on the piano and pick your 2nd string. Then bring it up to pitch in the same way. The other strings should be tackled in a similar manner, one by one. You will probably find that by the time you have reached the 6th string the higher ones have gone slightly off tune again. The reason for this is that the tension on the neck and belly of the instrument have been increased by the process of tuning the other strings, thus slackening off the ones tuned first. This means you will have re-adjust their tuning again slightly.

So much for tuning with a piano – *but you may not*

have a piano.

TUNING WITH PITCH PIPES

Another, more portable alternative is to tune to pitch pipes. Most music shops will have in stock a set of six small pipes which are tuned to the open strings of the guitar. If not, they should be able to supply you with a single one, in which case a G is the best note. With this G you can first tune your 3rd string, then tune the others from it by the process of relative tuning.

RELATIVE TUNING

This is by far the most efficient method of ensuring that your guitar is in tune with itself – which for playing on your own, is far more important than any considerations of perfect concert pitch. Relative tuning works by matching the sounds of adjacent strings, as follows: Having tuned the 3rd (G) string to your satisfaction, press your finger down on this string just behind the fourth fret and pick the string. Then, keeping your left-hand finger on the 3rd string, so that it will sustain the note, pick the open 2nd (B) string.

The sound produced by the 2nd string should be identical with that from the 3rd string stopped at the fourth fret, because you have shortened the length of the

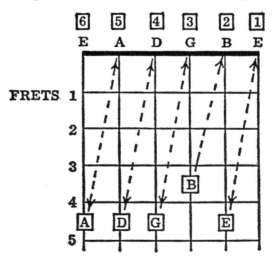

Relative Tuning Diagram

22

vibrating part of the 3rd string by four frets and raised its pitch four semitones – i.e. up to the note B. If the 2nd string isn't in tune, then it must be adjusted until it is identical. I must point out at this stage that when counting frets you should not include the nut – that is, the bar of hard wood, or ivory which is situated at the top of the fingerboard. All the musical vibration of a string takes place between the natural boundary points formed by this nut and the bridge. You will find both of these parts of the instrument indicated in the diagram on page 10.

When you are satisfied with the tuning of the open 2nd string, stop this string at the fifth fret, thus raising its pitch to E – and match it up with the 1st string in the same way. Now that your first three strings are in tune, go back to your 4th string and press it down at the fifth fret. This should sound in unison with your already tuned 3rd string. If it doesn't, adjust it accordingly, remembering that this time you should adjust the lower string – *not the higher one, which you have already tuned.*

When your 4th string is in tune, stop the 5th string at the fifth fret and match it with the 4th in the same way. Then the 6th string, which is stopped at the fifth fret also. You will probably find more difficulty in matching the pitch of these lower strings, but you'll improve with practice.

The illustration above shows in diagrammatic form the process which I have just explained. It is useful to remember that in each case – *with the sole exception of the 3rd string* – the equivalent note is made by stopping the lower string at the *fifth fret.*

It may seem to you that I've made rather a big thing of this business of tuning, but I can assure you that the operation is of primary importance if you are to make music on the guitar. As you progress you will find that your ear will develop and it will take you less and less time to achieve a tuning that satisfies you. But, however long it takes, never skimp on this most necessary task.

ELECTRONIC TUNERS
I've saved the best until last in the matter of Tuning,

23

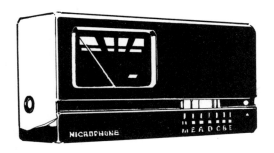

because I feel that as a beginner it is important that you develop your own ear. With the new Electronic Tuners you can tune a guitar into perfect pitch even if you can't hear it! This can be particularly useful for anyone who plays in a group, where there is sometimes quite a bit of noise going on and several people trying to tune up at the same time.

All you have to do with one of these tuners is to adjust your strings one by one, centreing the meter needle up on the dial of the gadget each time, and when you have done all six the guitar will be in tune. (Unless of course, a string has slipped after tuning – but it's easy enough to check on that.)

There are a number of Electronic Tuners on the market priced from about £20 upwards – which might sound quite a bit of money for such a routine job, but I can assure you they are well worth every penny. Consider for example my present group, with Bass guitar and two guitars. This involves 16 individual strings, each of which must be in perfect tune if we are going to produce a pleasant sound. Under the old system we usually got there finally, by adjusting to each other as we went along. But there were some nights – and this happens to everybody – when it just didn't come right and everybody ended up rather disgruntled. Now we all begin by using the same tuner and the old hassles are a thing of the past.

PLAYING POSITION
In the classical guitar stance the player sits on a chair, with his left foot resting flat on a stool and his right on the ground. The waist of the guitar can then rest natu-

rally on his horizontal thigh and is steadied in this position by the right forearm, which hangs naturally over the hips of the instrument.

The natural position of the left hand is found by bringing the hand up, with the palm facing away from you, until the thumb is in the middle of the back of the neck of the instrument and roughly parallel with it. The fingers are then arched round the neck so that they make contact with the strings at right angles. In this way, the pressures between the thumb and fingers balance each other.

Left Hand Position

This playing position has been developed over many years as both the most comfortable and the most efficient method of holding the guitar. I use it for both finger style and plectrum playing.

An alternative to the classic playing position, which does away with the need for a footstool, is to sit with the left leg crossed over the right, then rest the waist of the guitar on the left thigh, as before. This is the commonly used dance band guitarist's position. Whether or not it suits you is a matter of physical proportion between yourself and your guitar – BUT it is essential to remember that the instrument should *not* depend at all on your left hand for support. The left hand must be completely free to move up and down the fingerboard. To further ensure this freedom, take careful note of the angle of the neck, which should bring the head of the guitar up in line with the shoulder. This enables the player to reach any position on the fingerboard without any physical contortion.

Illustration of Classic Stance

At this point you may be saying: 'This is all very well, but all the groups I've seen, play standing up.' You're quite right. But the reason they do this has more to do with presentation than with music. In the pop world of today a guitarist is expected to perform a dance routine and assorted acrobatics in addition to playing his instrument. Fair enough, but you will find later on that difficult technical passages are much easier to play when you're sitting down than they are in the standing position. You'll hardly ever find a jazz guitarist playing standing up, and a classic player *never*. The technique of guitar playing is difficult enough, without making it harder for yourself.

But you still want to play standing up, because that's what the big beat groups do? All right. But let's do it the best way, eh? First you need a sling for your guitar. These range from a simple piece of braided cord up to a magnificent bull choker arrangement or ornately tooled leather. You pays your money you takes your choice, but if you're going to be playing standing up all night, a sling with a decently padded shoulder piece will be the most comfortable.

The best way of playing standing up is to adjust the sling so that the guitar is brought into a position as near as possible to that obtained in the sitting position. That is, the instrument should not dangle somewhere around your knees, but be held up on your chest. AND MOST IMPORTANT – the neck should be held well up, so that the head of the guitar is again in line with your shoulder.

THE PLECTRUM

I would recommend that you begin by using a plectrum to strike the strings. This is the easiest way in which a reasonable sound can be produced, and the only practical method for a metal strung instrument. Later on, in Chapter Fourteen, we will talk about the use of the right-hand fingers for striking the strings, in Spanish guitar playing.

The plectrum should be held between the thumb and forefinger of the right hand, as shown in the diagram. It is important that the forefinger should be crooked,

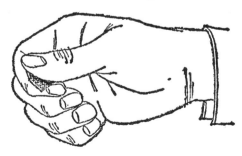

Illustration of Plectrum Holding Position

27

not straight, so that the plectrum balances on its first joint, held in place by the pressure of the thumb. Don't grasp the plectrum like grim death. Your grip should be firm, but relaxed.

The plectrum should move up and down across the strings, maintaining as nearly as possible an angle of 90° in relation to them. It is as well to practice at first with DOWN strokes only. After this technique has been mastered, you can then start practising UP strokes.

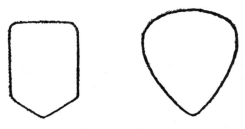

Plectrum Shapes

Plectrums come in a fantastic variety of shapes and sizes, and a great deal of personal taste enters into which type you should select. I find the two shapes shown below to be the most practical for me – the one on the left for solo playing and the one on the right for rhythm or accompaniment. Both are made of tortoiseshell, which gives a clearer, more brilliant tone than composition or plastic. A plectrum should have a certain flexibility, but not be too flimsy, otherwise the tone it produces will be correspondingly thin.

After a time you will naturally develop a preference for one particular shape, but I would suggest that you start out using the rhythm type illustrated above.

STRINGS

A lot of players, not all of them beginners, take strings for granted. For them, the only reason for replacing a string is that it has broken. They go on indefinitely playing on strings that are discoloured and rusty, their coverings frayed and loose. And they wonder why they cannot produce a good tone!

Give your instrument a chance. Strings are literally its vocal chords, and the best guitar in the world won't sound good if it isn't strung properly. In the course of being played strings pick up dirt, grease and perspiration from the fingers of even the most fastidious player. I would not dream of picking up a guitar with dirty hands, but during the course of a three or four hour session, especially if the weather is warm or the room over-heated, everybody's hands perspire and some of that must end up on the strings.

I *always* wipe the strings of my guitar with a duster kept especially for that purpose after a playing session. Even so the underside of the plain strings picks up dirt and corrosion, and the covered strings absorb the same stuff in between the windings where it is impossible to wipe off. Imperceptibly at first, this deposit begins to dull the sound of the strings, getting gradually worse and worse as it accumulates. Added to this is the fact that after a time the action of the metal frets on the covered strings will cause them to fray. This will interfere with pitch and cause them to buzz.

They should never be allowed to deteriorate to that degree, and this is one of the reasons why I say that you should not wait until a string breaks before replacing it. In fact, unless you're a very muscular player or just unlucky, you'll find that strings, particularly metal ones, break very seldom. Nylon strings have a habit of popping off during some quiet moment with a sound like a pistol shot and scaring the life out of you, because they are more sensitive to atmospheric changes.

It's not usually good policy to replace a single string. If one breaks that should be taken a cue to replace the entire set. In any case, whether a string breaks or not, if you're playing regularly the whole set should be replaced at least every couple of months. When you do this you will notice the difference immediately, even though you weren't aware how dead your old strings were before.

A new set of strings will cost you anything from £3 upwards, depending on the make you prefer, but you will find that the improvement in tonal brilliance is well worth the outlay. By the way, do make sure that you put on a matched set of strings – not oddments. Strings of different makes vary in gauge and tone and the introduction of 'strangers' can upset the action, the balance and the response of your guitar.

29

What make of string should you use? Well, this is a matter of personal taste, and you will have to find out by trial and error the strings that suit your instrument and your particular style of playing. There is a bewildering variety of makes and types of string on the market today so you should find something to suit you.

String Gauges are usually given in 1000ths of an inch. Broadly speaking most Rock players prefer a very light gauge with the First string an 8 or 9. This makes for a very easy action and loose strings which can be 'pulled' as much as a tone up from their normal pitch. Although I can see their advantages for some people I personally cannot play happily on this type of stringing and prefer a First string with a 12 gauge, which is tauter and gives more resistance and bounce to the plectrum. Barney Kessel, who plays with more bounce than anybody you'll ever hear, uses a 14 gauge First string, by the way.

There is a great variety of makes to choose from, but you won't go far wrong with Gibson, D'Addario, Fender or La Bella – each of which are available in at least four different gauges.

For the spanish guitar I still prefer Savarez Red Card, their high tension (heavy gauge) string. Savarez also make a super-high tension, Yellow Card set, but although they undoubtedly have a superb tone I don't feel this is worth the sacrifice in flexibility and left hand finger comfort.

A special note on 3rd strings. In the earlier edition of this book I recommended the use of a covered 3rd string on metal strung guitars, because in those days uncovered 3rd strings tended to play out of tune. Due to improvements in manufacture this condition no longer applies, and I have been quite happily using plain 3rds for some time on my metal strung guitars as well as on my nylon strung instruments.

These are just some of the bare bone facts about the guitar that you ought to know. You'll pick up a lot more as you go through this book. But right now you must be anxious to start playing. So, if you've tuned your instrument, let's turn to Section Two and get on with it!

Chapter Four
CHORDS IN G

THE THREE-CHORD TRICK

The guitar is an ideal accompanying instrument, and the easiest and most satisfying manner in which to begin learning to play is to take advantage of this fact. In this section I shall show you how to use your guitar to accompany a number of well-known folk songs, and you should be able to start making satisfying musical sounds within a very short time.

These sounds will be chords – which are defined in my dictionary as 'a simultaneous and harmonious union of sounds of different pitch'. In guitar terms this means simply three or more strings played at the same time. Chords are the basis of all guitar technique, and they are particularly important in accompaniment playing because of the fullness of the sound they provide. So you must begin to learn chords and the chord symbol system, which is a very useful form of musical shorthand with many uses.

In every musical key there are three principal chords, which are known as the tonic, the dominant and the sub-dominant. In the key of G these three chords are G, D7 (pronounced D seventh) and C, and you will find them used in different permutations and with additions throughout the accompaniment of any song written in this key. It follows logically that the more complicated the harmony of a song, the greater the number of additional chords required, but most folk songs have a simple harmonic structure and in many cases they can be accompanied quite satisfactorily by using nothing more than the three principal chords mentioned above.

THE CHORD WINDOW SYSTEM

The best way for a beginner to learn his chords is

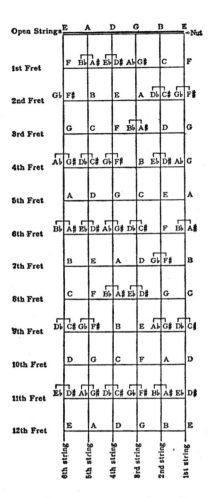

*The Guitar Fingerboard
with Names of Notes*

through a system of diagrams known as 'windows'. (The origin of this name will soon become obvious.) The window system is based on a pictorial representation of the guitar fingerboard as shown below.

The vertical lines represent the strings of the guitar, 6th, 5th, 4th and so on, reading from left to right. I have shown the top horizontal line as a double one, to indicate that it represents the nut – that is the point which

32

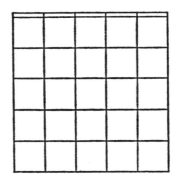

**Chord Window
No Fingering**

divides the vibrating section of the strings from the part which goes on to the tuning head. As you will see from the diagram of the guitar fingerboard on the opposite page, the frets are numbered downwards, 1st, 2nd, 3rd and so on. To show a chord in the window system it is merely necessary to add its fingering to the basic diagram. Thus the first of our principal chords G is as shown below.

The circle on the 1st string shows the position at which the string should be pressed. The number inside the circle indicates that the third finger of the left hand should be used for this purpose – *no other*. It is important at this stage that you should use precisely the left-hand fingering indicated. To keep things as simple as possible I have given you only the four-string chord of G. Later on, when you learn the additional left-hand fingering that makes this chord into a six-string one, you may encounter unnecessary difficulty if you get into the habit of using the wrong fingers now.

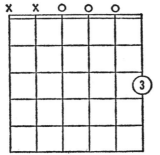

Chord Window G

33

Over the nut position on the diagram you will notice the two symbols X and O. These refer to the un-fingered strings in the chord shape. When X is placed over a string, this string should *not* be sounded. Therefore, in the example above, the 5th and 6th strings are not played. The O symbol placed over a string means that, although it is not fingered, the string should be sounded. In this case you will see that the 4th, 3rd and 2nd strings are played open in this way, producing the notes D, G and B, which are in fact the basic notes of the chord of G.

When fingering a string it should be pressed down just *behind*, NOT on the fret. This brings the string firmly into contact with the metal of the fret, thus shortening the length of the part which vibrates when struck and making its pitch higher than that of the open string. In this case the 1st (E) string is stopped at the third fret and becomes G. If you turn back to the Fingerboard Diagram at the beginning of this section you will be able to check this. Notice that each time you move your finger up a fret, the pitch of the string goes up a semitone.

Now, holding your plectrum between the first finger and thumb of the right hand, as described earlier, draw it cross the top four strings. Remember, *just the top four* – we are not using the 5th and 6th string at this stage. You should not have any difficulty in producing a musical sound from the 4th, 3rd and 2nd strings in this chord, because they are sounded open, but you may find that the 1st gives you nothing more than an inelegant 'phut'. This does not indicate that there is anything wrong with your guitar, or with the method of fingering described above. The trouble lies in the fact that at this stage your fingers are not strong enough, nor your finger-ends hard enough, to press the strings down with sufficient firmness. Another possible fault is that the side of your left-hand finger may be making accidental contact with the un-fingered 2nd string and deadening its sound.

DON'T get discouraged and say: 'My fingers will never be strong enough' or 'My fingers are too big and clumsy to play the guitar'. You'll be surprised how smart your fingers can become in time, if you give them the chance of practice and exercise. Always remember that you should use the harder, tips of your fingers, rather than the fleshy forepart – check again on the Left Hand Position diagram in Chapter Three.

Your finger-ends will become sore, and if you're practising as you should, they'll remain sore for weeks on end. But this will wear off in time, as you develop hard pads of skin at the finger-ends. *This point alone makes nonsense of any claim to teach guitar playing in a day, or a week* – the actual process of physical adaptation takes time, and there is no way of avoiding the fact.

A SPECIAL NOTE FOR THE LADIES
You're going to have to cut those lovely long finger-nails on your left hand. If you don't you'll never be able to press the strings down in the correct manner. So get out the clippers and look upon it as a sacrifice made for your Art.

THE OTHER PRINCIPAL CHORDS IN G
The dominant seventh chord in this key is D7. This time we'll use a *five*-string chord, because both the 4th and 5th strings can be played open.

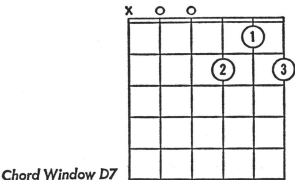

Chord Window D7

Finger this chord, using left-hand fingers indicated in the window. Then play it slowly, one string after another, to make sure that each is sounding properly. If it isn't, look again at your left-hand fingers, to see if you are pressing the strings down with sufficient firmness, and in the correct position behind the frets. Also check in case any of your fingers are fouling adjacent strings and preventing them from vibrating.

When you feel happy about D7, try changing from D7 to G . . . and back again. It will be a struggle at first. You'll find it necessary to look down at the fingerboard and guide your left-hand fingers carefully into position. Don't worry – we've all been through this stage, and the only way to get past it is to practise the change again and again until you are able to make it smoothly. Don't worry about speed, just take it slow and easy, and make sure that all the notes in each chord sound *every time*.

The other principal chord in the key, the sub-dominant, is C, which is shown below in a four-string version.

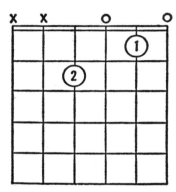

Chord Window C

The 5th and 6th strings are not sounded in this chord, as you will note from the X symbols above the nut position. The O symbol over the 1st and 3rd strings indicates that they should be played open. When you have mastered the C chord, try changing from this to D7, and then to G.

A NOTE ON TONE PRODUCTION

Concentrate from the outset on making as full a sound as possible each time you play a chord. By this I don't mean that you should bash the plectrum down on the strings with all the force you can muster. This will only succeed in producing ugly rattles and buzzes. It is far more important at this stage – and at any other, for that matter – that you should obtain the best tone of which your instrument is capable, rather than striving for sheer volume.

You will no doubt have noticed by now that the position at which you strike the strings makes a distinct difference to the nature of the tone produced. If you haven't already done so, experiment with this. Finger the G chord with your left hand and strike the strings close to the bridge. The tone thus produced will be bright and tinny – almost banjo-like. Now, still holding the chord, move your right hand up past the sound-hole to where the neck joins the body of the instrument and draw the plectrum slowly across the strings at this position. The tone this time will be softer, but much rounder and more mellow.

As with so many things, the happy medium is the one to be recommended. That is, a playing position about half-way between these two extremes. This leaves the very sharp and very mellow tones in reserve for any special effects you may wish to produce.

STRUMMING AND ARPEGGIOS
When the plectrum is drawn quickly across the strings all the notes of a chord sound more or less simultaneously. This is strumming, in which you will not normally be able to distinguish one note from another, but are aware of the chord as a blended whole. If on the other hand, you draw the plectrum across the strings more slowly, so that there is a definite time lag between one note and the next, you will produce what is known as an arpeggio.

The strumming, rhythmic style is the one we shall use for our accompaniments at first. It is therefore important that you should learn to strum with a regular beat, in order to make your accompaniment as rhythmic as possible. Try fingering the G chord with your left hand and strumming, counting an even 1-2-3-4 as you do so.

After the chord symbols – such as the C, D7, G we have learned so far – diagonal lines like this / are used to indicate how many times the chord should be repeated. Thus the 1-2-3-4 beats on the chord of G which you have just played are written in symbol notation| G / / /| The vertical lines are Bar lines. In the example here you will be playing a four to the bar rhythm. You will also find that a lot of pieces are written in three to the bar rhythm, or waltz time. Three to the bar looks like this| G / /| and is counted 1-2-3, 1-2-3 and so on.

Now that you are reasonably familiar with the fingering of the three principal chords in G, try the following exercise over a few times to get used to changing from one chord to another.

Play four beats to the bar, strumming:

||: G / / / | C / / / | D7 / / / | G / / / :||

The double lines and dots at the beginning and end of this exercise || : :|| indicate that the section enclosed by them should be repeated. Remember this, as you will encounter them often in the future. In this instance you should repeat the exercise until you are sure that you can hit the chords correctly each time and maintain a constant rhythm. In all exercises it is better to start off quite slowly, at a tempo you can manage easily without fumbling the changes. If the first part of an exercise seems easy, many students have a tendency to begin as fast as they can – only to come a cropper when something more difficult turns up later on. This is bad because it produces a chopping and changing of the original tempo which robs the exercise of any musical value whatsoever. Go slowly at first, concentrating on producing a good tone and a full sound. Speed doesn't matter at this stage. That will come naturally with practice. Maintaining a steady tempo is much more important.

Now let's try our first folk song, GOODNIGHT LADIES, which uses the chords of G. The starting note for this song is the open 2nd string (B). In fact, if you like, you can pick out the melody of the first two bars completely on open strings, by playing in this order: 2nd, 3rd, 4th, 3rd. This gives you the notes equivalent to the phrase 'Goodnight Ladies'. Play it over a couple of times to get the idea before going on to the song.

STRUM FOUR TO THE BAR
BEAT FOUR TO THE BAR

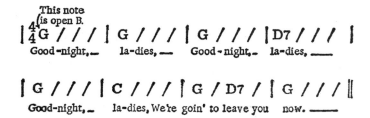

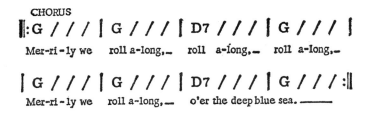

You may have noticed that the last chord of the song is G, the tonic chord. The tonic is sometimes referred to as the 'home' chord, because it is invariably the one upon which a piece written in a particular key ends. Thus, a song played in the key of G will end on the chord of G, or one in the key of G will end on the chord of G, or one in the key of C, on the chord of C.

Now, if you've studied this chapter and played the examples over a few times you've got a reasonable idea of the basic chords in the key of G. Chances are that you've also acquired a set of sore left-hand fingers, so put your guitar away for the time being. However much you try, you're not going to learn everything in one session. Next time it will be easier, and the time after that easier still.

Whatever you do, *don't* be discouraged because playing the guitar isn't quite as easy as you expected it to be before you took the plunge. If you are feeling a bit down, then play a record of your favourite guitarist – *and remind yourself that he was once at precisely the same stage you are now.* And after all, he's only human, isn't he?

Chapter Five

CHORDS IN C

The next simple and frequently used key for accompaniments is C. Here again we have a set of three principal chords. This time C is the tonic, or home chord. The dominant is G7, and the sub-dominant is F. You've already learned the four-string version of the chord of C in the previous chapter, so you're part of the way there. However, this time we're going to use the *six*-string version, which looks like this:

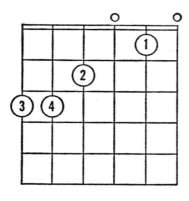

Chord Window C
(six string)

Your first and second fingers go on the 2nd and 4th strings in the same positions as before, but now we are adding the fourth finger on the third fret of the 5th string and the third finger on the third fret of the 6th string. You won't do this perfectly the first time, but will become easier with practice. Try moving from this version on to the other chords that you know already – and back again. Like this: ||: C / / / | D7 / / / | C / / / | G / / / :||

Now we can move on to the sub-dominant of the key, G7. The four-string version of this is probably the easiest chord there is to play on the guitar. It requires only the use of your first finger left hand. The other three notes of the chord are formed naturally by the open 2nd, 3rd and 4th strings, as you will see from the window below.

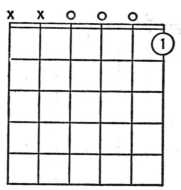

Chord Window G7
(four string)

40

It shouldn't take you long to get this one, but here again the important thing is to be able to move as quickly as possible from the fingering of one chord to another, so you should try practising something like the following:

||: G7 / / / | C / / / | G7 / / / | C / / / :||

We talked in the last chapter about the three chord trick, but here's something even easier – a song accompaniment that uses only two chords. The song is OH DEAR! WHAT CAN THE MATTER BE? and I've written out the chords and words below. You may be familiar with certain variations on this lyric, but whether you use them or not depends on you, and your audience, if any.

The melody of the song begins on the note G, which is the sound of your open 3rd string, so hit that note first

to give you a guide for pitching your voice. Then strum a bright, lilting three to a bar rhythm.

So now you know four chords and you can play two complete song accompaniments. But don't rush out and sign that TV contract just yet. There's still another chord to learn in the key of C, and feeling very pleased with yourself after your vocal effort, you should be in just the mood to tackle it. The chord is F, and it is illustrated below in window form.

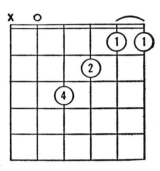

Chord Window F
(five string)

Yes, it is a bit of a stinker, isn't it? But don't panic. You'll notice that in this chord the first finger stops both the 1st and 2nd strings, which means that you can't use the tip of the finger as before. Instead, the first finger is flattened down to bring its first joint in line with the fingerboard. Try that first, picking the 1st and 2nd strings only. If the strings don't ring, adjust the position of your finger until they do. Take your time. Then when you're certain you've mastered this part of the chord, place your second finger on the 3rd string at the second fret, still keeping your first finger in position. Now pick the 3rd, 2nd and 1st strings in that order.

When those three are sounding clearly, you can then add the fourth note, which is made by placing your fourth finger on the third fret of the 4th string. Now play all four strings – arpeggio fashion at first to make sure they're all ringing as they should – then five strings, by including your un-fingered 5th – then strum.

When you've mastered the F chord on its own, try changing between it and the other chords in the key, something like this:

‖: F / / / | G7 / / / | F / / / | C / / / :‖

I can't emphasise too much how important it is to learn to change quickly from one chord to another. Each chord is a building block, and its shape has to be learned individually, but to play a chord sequence like that given above, without stumbling or hesitating between the bar lines, it is neecessary to go on practising until the left-hand fingers move automatically to the correct position on seeing a given symbol.

A good quotation to remember at this point is one by Hazlitt, who said: 'We never do anything well till we cease to think about the manner of doing it.' That is what we are aiming for, to be able to finger chords without having to 'think about the manner of doing it'. I know that seems to be asking a great deal at this stage, but I assure you that if you persevere with your practice you will succeed in reaching this goal.

Our next song is ON TOP OF OLD SMOKY, and the starting note is C. You can find this on the 2nd string at the first fret. In fact, if you play two of these Cs, followed by your open E string, you've got the *first three* notes of the tune. By the way, we're in three to the bar rhythm again, so count 1-2-3.

This note is C ↳On 3/4 F / / | F / / | F / / |
                     top of Old Smok - y, ————

| F / / | F / / | C / / | G7 / / |
———— All cov-ered with snow, ————

| C / / | C / / | G7 / / | G7 / / |
———— I lost my true lov • er ————

| G7 / / | G7 / / | C / / | F / / ‖
———— For court-in' too slow. ————

| C / / | C / / | F / / | F / / |
———— A thief will just rob ———— you ————

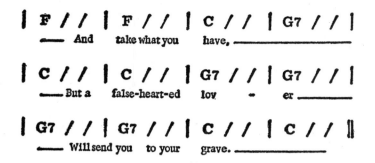

| F / / | F / / | C / / | G7 / / |
— And　take what you　have, ——

| C / / | C / / | G7 / / | G7 / / |
— But a　false-heart-ed　lov • er ———

| G7 / / | G7 / / | C / / | C / / ‖
— Will send you　to your　grave. ———

SIX-STRING CHORDS

Now let's try the six-string version of G7, which looks like this:

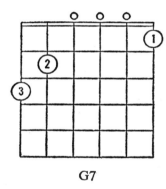

G7

The 1st string is stopped at the first fret as before, but added to this we have the second finger on the second fret of the 5th string and the third finger on the third fret of the 6th string. Try this, and make sure that all the strings sound by playing an arpeggio.

It will well repay you to give serious study to this matter of six-string chords, because they can give a much greater depth to your accompaniments with their 'bassy' sound. Where six-string chords are not practical, try for five, bearing in mind all the time the idea of getting as full a sound as possible from your instrument.

The chords you have been learning so far are all in the first position, which means that you are playing basically on the first three frets. This enables you to use open string notes where available. The advantage of this is that the left-hand fingering of such chords is

44

simpler than it would be in higher positions, where all the strings that are sounded would to be fingered. The aim at the moment is to get you playing reasonably full-sounding song accompaniments, and this is best done with first position chords. Later on you may go on to learn that there are – for instance – ten different positions and ways of fingering the simple chord of C, but there's no need to worry about that at the moment.

Now let's have a re-cap of the chords you have already learned, with windows showing them in the fullest practical form for you at the present time.

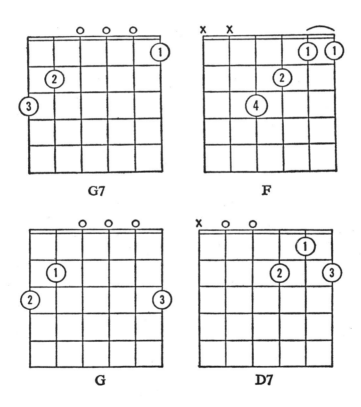

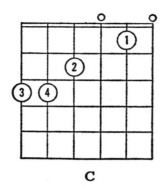

C

From the above you will see that you already have in your repertoire three six-string and two five-string chords. Play them one by one, taking your time and making sure that you know their fingerings.

Now here's another song, using the chords of C, G7 and F. The song is MY BONNIE LIES OVER THE OCEAN, and you'll find the first two notes of the melody if you play the open 3rd and 1st strings, in that order. This song is in three to a bar, a bright waltz time.

This note is open G

$\frac{3}{4}$ C | C / / | C / / | C / / |
My bon - nie lies o - ver the o - cean,___

| C / / | C / / | C / / | G7 / / |
___ My bon-nie lies o-ver the sea; ___

| G7 / / | C / / | C / / | C / / |
___ My bon-nie lies o-ver the o - cean,___

| C / / | F / / | G7 / / | C / / ‖
___ Oh bring back my bon-nie to me. ___

Chorus

‖: C / / | C / / | F / / | F / / |
Bring ___ back, ___ bring ___ back,___ Oh

46

| G7 / / | G7 / / | C / / | C / / |
bring back my   bon - nie to   me,_ to   me, ___

| C / / | C / / | F / / | F / / |
Bring ___   back, ___   bring___   back,_ Oh

| G7 / / | G7 / / | C / / | C / / :‖
bring back my   bon - nie to   me. _____

And now, going back to your chords in G, let's try THE BLUE TAIL FLY. You can find the first three notes of the melody by playing on your 2nd string like this: open, first fret, open - the notes B, C, B. This song is played at an easy four to the bar.

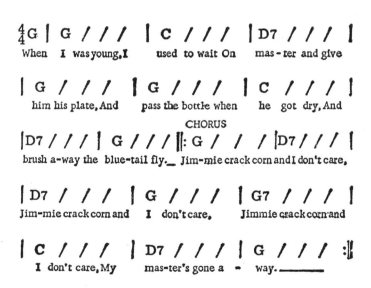

⁴⁄₄ G | G / / / | C / / / | D7 / / / |
When I was young, I   used to wait On   mas - ter and give

| G / / / | G / / / | C / / / |
him his plate, And   pass the bottle when   he got dry, And

CHORUS

| D7 / / / | G / / / ‖: G / / / | D7 / / / |
brush a-way the blue-tail fly._ Jim-mie crack corn and I don't care,

| D7 / / / | G / / / | G7 / / / |
Jim-mie crack corn and   I don't care,   Jimmie crack corn and

| C / / / | D7 / / / | G / / / :‖
I don't care, My   mas-ter's gone a - way. _____

47

Chapter Six

CHORDS IN D

When Eddie Lang, the first great jazz guitarist, played with the Paul Whiteman Orchestra back in the early 1930s the story that he carried his band parts written on a piece of card about the size of an average business card became something of a legend. If the story is true, it must be an example of the kind of thing that is possible through the use of the chord symbol system, which you are in the process of learning.

My own adaptation of Eddie Lang's business card – one which I have found useful over many years – involves the use of an ordinary pocket-sized, indexed address book. You can buy one of these from a stationers quite cheaply and start to build your own library of chord accompaniments today. Write out the chord symbols – and the words of the song too, if you like – as I have done in these chapters, and you'll be surprised how quickly you can build up a range of songs to suit all occasions. Why not start with the accompaniments you'll find in this book?

Our next three chords are in the key of D. They are D, the tonic, A7 the dominant, and the G the sub-dominant. Your 'bonus' chord here is G, which is carried over from the previous chapter, so once again you really only have *two* chords to learn.

The five string chord of D in the first position looks like this:

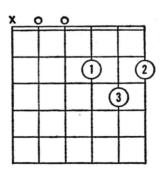

Chord Window D

You will notice here that the 4th and 5th strings are played open, giving you a ringing, sonorous bass sound. Try the chord, making sure you use the left-hand fingers indicated. Play arpeggio first, to make sure of those first three strings.

The Dominant Seventh in the key is A7, an extremely useful chord shape. This employs for the first time in your experience the *Small Barré* – that is, the use of the first finger to hold down the 2nd, 3rd and 4th strings simultaneously. At the same time, the third finger is used to press the 1st string down at the third fret. The 5th and 6th strings can be sounded open in this chord, giving a good ringing bass once again.

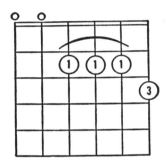

Chord Window A7

The G chord you already know, so let's try a small exercise, using the three chords in D.

||⁴ D / / / | G / / / | A7 / / / | D / / / :||

Repeat this until you have the feel of changing between these chords . . . until your fingers are so educated that you don't have to watch what they're doing.

Now, if you're happy about those changes, we'll play one of the most beautiful songs ever written, Stephen Foster's OLD FOLKS AT HOME. To find the first three notes of the melody, finger the D chord and hit your first string, then raise your second finger and allow the open 1st string to sound, then the 2nd string, with your third finger on the third fret, as in the D chord. This gives you: *Way down u-* the notes F sharp, E and D. The song is played in a slow four to the bar. Whatever you do don't play the accompaniment jerkily. This is a good time to try a sustained, arpeggio type of accompaniment, letting the strings ring behind the melody.

‖⁴₄ D / D7 / | G / / / | D / / / | A7 / / / |

'Way down upon the Swanee River,_ Far,_ far a • way, ___

| D / D7 / | G / / / | D / A7 / | D / / / |

There's where turning ev-er, There's where stay. ___
my heart is the old folks

| D / D7 / | G / / / | D / / / | A7 / / / |

All up and down old cre-a-tion Sad - ly I roam, ___
the

| D / D7 / | G / / / | D / A7 / | D / / / ‖

Still look-ing for old plan-ta-tion,And for the old home. __
the folks at
CHORUS

‖: A7 / / / | D / / / | G / / / | D / / / |

All the world is sad and dreary, Ev-ry-where I roam. __

| D / D7 / | G / / / | D / A7 / | D / / / :‖

Oh,darkies how my heart grows Far from the old home. __
wear-y, folks at

An interesting point to note about this piece is the way the chords progress – that is, the way the D moves to D7 and then to G. This is a very common type of chord progression, but it has a beautiful logic of its own that will become more and more apparent as you listen to it. The study of chord progression will come to you naturally as you learn more about the guitar, and you will begin to learn the non-academic kind of finger-board harmony which becomes instinctive to guitarists.

You will remember that I mentioned in Chapter Four that a song invariably ends on the tonic chord – in this case D. Alongside this you can place another rule of thumb – not invariable, but useful to bear in mind as a guide. The dominant chord is *usually* followed by the tonic chord. Thus, in the present piece, the resolution of the A7 to D at the end of the song. The term *Resolution* in music merely means a natural movement of the harmony towards a musical conclusion. As such, it is immediately recognizable to the ear as satisfactory; whereas an un-resolved progression has the lack of coherence of a broken off sentence in speech.

As you play more and more you will begin to recognize the pattern of chord progressions of songs, so that you will be able to play a reasonably correct accompaniment to a song without ever having seen the chords written down. But you will only do this if you have first learned your basic chords. They are the building blocks, so stick at it!

An example of a commonly used chord progression is the 12-bar blues:

$\|\mathbin{:}\frac{4}{4}$ D / / / | D / / / | D / / / | D7 / / / |

| G / / / | G / / / | D / / / | D / / / |

| A7 / / / | A7 / / / | D / / / | D / / / :$\|$

The next song is FRANKIE AND JOHNNY, a 12-bar blues. The first note of the melody is D – your open 4th string.

| $\frac{4}{4}$ D / / / | D / / / | D / / / | D7 / / / |

Frankie and Johnny were sweet-hearts,— O. Lordy, how they could love! — They

| G / / / | G / / / | D / / / | D / / / |

swore to be true to each oth-er. —— True as the stars a - bove. He was her

| A7 / / / | A7 / / / | D / / / | D / / / ‖

man, —— But he done her wrong. ——

| D / / / | D / / / | D / / / | D7 / / / |

Frankie and Johnny went walk-ing, — Johnny in his brand new shirt, ——

| G / / / | G / / / | D / / / | D / / / |

O good Lord, says Fran-kie, — Don't my Johnny look cute? He was her

| A7 / / / | A7 / / / | D / / / | D / / / ‖

man, —— But he done her wrong. ——

The 12-bar blues is the basic harmony of any number of Negro songs, and later, a great deal of jazz. Listen to the recordings of any of the great blues singers, Bessie

Smith, for instance, you will hear this progression used again and again, in different keys and with slight variations. Don't forget that any of the progressions you may learn can be transposed and played in *any key* to suit the pitch of the singer. This isn't as difficult as it sounds, and we'll go into it later in more detail.

Now here is the 12-bar blues written in the other two keys with which you are already familiar – C and G. Play the progression over in each key and sing the FRANKIE AND JOHNNY melody – you'll find that it fits perfectly. The point about this exercise is to show you that the relationships of the chords within the progression are the same, whatever key you're playing them in. To put it in equation form: C is to G7 as G is to D7, as D is to A7. You can find the first note of FRANKIE AND JOHNNY each time by playing the tonic note.

Before you can play the 12-bar blues in C, you're going to need another chord: C7

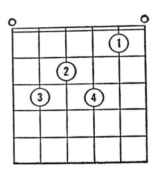

Chord Window C7

Now, the 12-bar blues in C:

$\|{}^{4}_{4}$ C / / / | C / / / | C / / / | C7 / / / |

| F / / / | F / / / | C / / / | C / / / |

| G7 / / / | G7 / / / | C / / / | C / / / :‖

And in G:

$\|{}^{4}_{4}$ G / / / | G / / / | G / / / | G7 / / / |

52

| C / / / | C / / / | G / / / | G / / / |

| D7 / / / | D7 / / / | G / / / | G / / / :||

Chapter Seven
CHORDS IN A

A is a favourite key of many of the classical composers for the guitar. One good reason for this is the fact that the 5th and 6th strings are tuned to the natural bass notes of the key - A and E, thus allowing these strings to be played open as accompaniment to more complicated fingering with the left hand. From our point of view this offers a good opportunity to begin to explore the string bass style of playing.

The string bass style means merely that, having formed a chord with your left hand, instead of strumming it straight across, or playing it arpeggio fashion, you hit one of the lower strings on its own for the first beat of the bar, then play the remainder of the chord on the second. You can then play another bass string, followed by the chord, for the third and fourth beats.

Thus, without moving your left hand from its chord shape, you can produce an *um - ching, um - ching*, sort of sound, which can be the ideal accompaniment for the country and western type of number. Many years ago, when I played with an outfit called Big Bill Campbell and his Rocky Mountain Rhythm (if you don't remember them, ask your dad) I used to play this kind of rhythm most of the time.

You may wonder why I didn't go stark, raving bonkers with the monotony of this *um - ching um - ching*, but it is possible to make this style very interesting both from the playing and listening points of view. If you can get hold of some of the old Eddie Land/Joe Venuti recordings you'll hear Lang using this type of accompaniment to good effect. Another example that falls immediately to mind is Django Reinhardt's duet version of ALABAMY BOUND, made with Stephen Grappelly in 1937 – I guarantee that the first time you listen to this one you just won't believe that there's only one guitar playing the accompaniment.

Just *how* interesting you can make the string bass style depends on your ability and imagination. By taking care in the choice of your bass notes you can produce a pleasant counter-melody to the song. *Don't try to play the tune itself* – a counter-melody should fill in the gaps, rather than competing or dominating. You'll get to play the melody yourself later on, but at the moment we're concentrating on the job of making a reasonable accompanist of you, and this is an art in itself. Your chance to become a soloist will come in Section Four.

Now, the principal chords in the key of A. These are A, E7 and D. As usual, we'll take the tonic chord first:

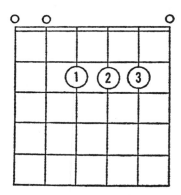

Chord Window A

By now your fingers should be becoming hard enough and flexible enough to find the correct position without much difficulty. Try this chord arpeggio fashion, making sure that the fingered 4th, 3rd and 2nd strings ring as well as the open ones. Now try playing the chord in the string bass style, hitting the open 5th string alone first, followed by the chord, then the open 6th, followed by the chord. *Um - ching, um - ching -* get it?

Now we'll try the dominant, which is E7 and looks like this:

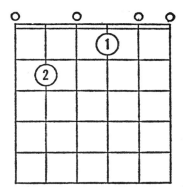

Chord Window E7

Try this chord in the same way, hitting the 5th string first, then the chord, then the 6th, followed by the chord. When you're sure you've got the idea, try the following exercise, which combines the use of the two chords. Play it in a steady four to the bar, string bass style.

$\left\|\frac{4}{4}\right.$ A / / / | A / / / | E7 / / / | E7 / / / |

| A / / / | E7 / / / | A / / / | A / / / $\|$

Now I would like to introduce you to the bar repeat sign /. You will come across this quite frequently in chord symbol writing. It merely means, repeat the previous bar. With its help, the exercise above would look like this:

$\left\|\frac{4}{4}\right.$ A / / / | ╱. | E7 / / / | ╱. |

| A / / / | E7 / / / | A / / / | ╱. $\|$

The third, sub-dominant chord in the key of A is the chord of D, which you have already learned. I'm going to give you a new diagram for this, using a slightly different fingering from before. This time you use a *Small Barré* with the first finger to hold down both the 1st and 3rd strings, like this:

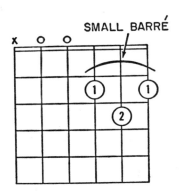

Chord Window D

Finger this chord, and play it in the string bass style, hitting the 4th string first, followed by the chord – then the 5th string, followed by the chord.

Now here's another song, using the chords you have learned in this chapter, plus A7. You can play string bass style on A7 by hitting the open 5th and 6th strings, as you do when playing A.

To find the first four notes of the melody – 'When I was a—', finger your A chord, then play the 4th string followed by the 3rd string *three* times. This gives you the notes E, A, A, A. the song is FOGGY FOGGY DEW. Play it in an easy four to the bar tempo, using the string bass style.

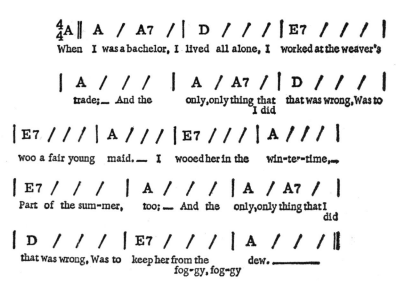

And now, in the same key, another old Western folk song RED RIVER VALLEY. The first three notes of this song are contained in the A chord, and you can find them by fingering A, then playing 4th, 3rd and 2nd strings, in that order. This song should be played four to the bar, but slightly slower than the last one.

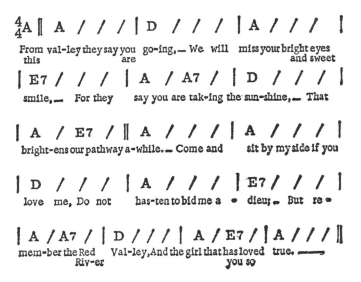

Chapter Eight

MINOR CHORDS AND

INTRODUCTIONS

The chords we have discussed so far have all been in major keys, and based on what are known as major triads. Each major key also has a relative minor key, which has a characteristic sound of its own. To show you this difference in sound, finger and play the following chords. First the A chord you have learned already:

57

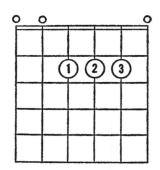

A Major Chord Window

And now the chord of A minor, which looks like this:

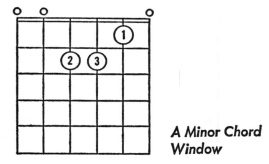

A Minor Chord Window

The only difference between these two chords is, as you will see, the fact that the 2nd string is fingered one fret lower in the minor chord. This makes the note on the 2nd string C *natural*, instead of C sharp. Although everything else about the chord remains unchanged, this minor third interval between the A on the 3rd string and C on the 2nd gives the chord its characteristic minor sound.

A minor is the relative minor key to C major. As with the major key, the minor key has three principal chords. Those in A minor are A minor, E7 and D minor. E7 you already know, as this is the *same* chord which is the dominant seventh in the key of A major.

D minor looks like this:

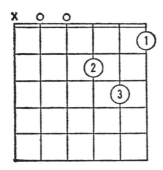

**Chord Window
D Minor**

Here again you will see that the only difference between D minor and the D major chord, which you have learned already, lies in one note. In this instance the 1st string is fingered one fret lower, putting an F natural at the top of the chord, instead of an F sharp.

In chord symbol writing A minor is usually written Am - or sometimes Amin, and D minor written Dm or Dmin, and so on through the minor chords.

Although only one note is changed in both of the minor chords we have discussed so far, you will notice that this necessitates a considerable modification of the fingering in each case. Thus we can improvise a useful exercise for your left hand by alternating major and minor chords, as follows:

|| ⁴₄ A / / / | Am / / / | D / / / | Dm / / / ||

Play this exercise very slowly at first, gaining speed as your left-hand fingers become more accustomed to the necessary movements.

Now you should be ready to play this simple exercise on the chords of A minor.

|| ⁴₄ Am / / / | Dm / / / | E7 / / / | Am / / / ||

Remember to take full advantage of the sound of the open strings—for instance in the Am chord, where the 5th and 6th can be sounded open.

The next minor key you will find useful is E minor, which is the relative minor to the key of G major. Its three principal chords are Em, B7 and Am.

Em is a very simple chord to finger, and it looks like this:

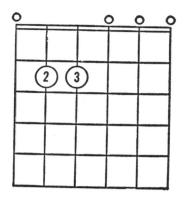

Chord Window
E Minor

Played arpeggio fashion across the strings, this chord will give you the full sonority of which your guitar is capable. Minor keys, particularly those in which the open strings can be used, are very effective on the guitar.

B7 is unfortunately, not quite so easy. It employs all four fingers of the left hand, and looks like this:

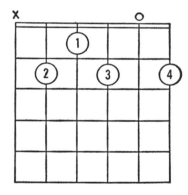

Chord Window B7

Spend a bit of time on this one, and don't worry too much if you don't get it right away. It will come with practice.

The third chord in the key of E minor is Am, which you already know, so now let's try a song accompaniment in the key of A Minor. The song is a beautiful old Russian one called DARK EYES. You can find the first three notes of the melody on the 4th string, by fingering the first fret, second fret and third fret, in that order – then move on to the E7 chord. The song is played in three to the bar, and sounds at its best when accompanied in arpeggio style with very little accent on the rhythm. The three notes I have given you above correspond to the words 'Ev-ry night . . .'

$$\frac{3}{4} \| \ \text{E7} \ / \ / \ | \quad \text{\slashed} \quad | \ \text{Am} \ / \ / \ |$$

1. Ev'-ry   night I dream ▬   Of two   dear, dark eyes ▬

$$| \ \text{Am} \ / \ / \ | \ \text{Dm E7} \ / \ | \ \text{E7} \ / \ / \ | \ \text{Am} \ / \ / \ |$$

▬ Like twin   stars that gleam ▬ When the   twi-light dies.▬

$$| \ \text{Am} \ / \ / \ | \ \text{Dm} \ / \ / \ | \quad \text{\slashed} \quad | \ \text{Am} \ / \ / \ |$$

▬ Love-light   made them glow ▬   In the   long a - go, ▬

$$| \ \text{Am} \ / \ / \ | \ \text{E7} \ / \ / \ | \quad \text{\slashed} \quad | \ \text{Am} \ / \ / \ |$$

▬ Oh, I   miss you so, ▬   Dear dark   eyes. ▬

$$| \ \text{Am} \ / \ / \ | \ \text{E7} \ / \ / \ | \quad \text{\slashed} \quad | \ \text{Am} \ / \ / \ |$$

2. Oh, come back, dark eyes ▬   For the   twi-light dies; ▬

$$| \ \text{Am} \ / \ / \ | \ \text{Dm E7} \ / \ | \ \text{E7} \ / \ / \ | \ \text{Am} \ / \ / \ |$$

▬ And the   stars a-bove ▬ Call fond   hearts to love.▬

$$| \ \text{Am} \ / \ / \ | \ \text{Dm} \ / \ / \ | \quad \text{\slashed} \quad | \ \text{Am} \ / \ / \ |$$

▬ But my   lone-ly heart ▬ Weeps while   we're a-part, ▬

$$| \ \text{Am} \ / \ / \ | \ \text{E7} \ / \ / \ | \quad \text{\slashed} \quad | \ \text{Am} \ / \ / \ \|$$

▬ For I   love you so, ▬   Dear dark   eyes. ▬

As I mentioned above, each major key has its relative minor key, but we're not going to go into all of them at this stage. The main thing I am trying to do in this section is to equip you to play accompaniments to songs in keys which can be managed easily in the first position. Later on, if you wish to, you can go on to learn the chords in *all* keys, but there's no reason why you shouldn't jog along quite happily with your accompaniments for quite a while yet, using only the chords you have learned so far.

Before we leave the subject of minor keys, however, it would be a good idea to give you one more set of three

61

chords. These are the chords in D minor, which is the relative minor to F major. They are Dm, A7 and Gm.

Dm you have already learned earlier in this chapter, but here's a reminder window:

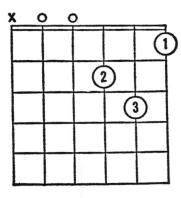

**Chord Window
D Minor**

The same applies to A7, which is of course the dominant 7th chord in the key of D major. But this time let's try a slightly different version of the chord. One which gives us more open strings.

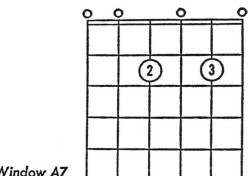

Chord Window A7

The other chord in this key, Gm is very simple in its four-string version, so we'll stick to that for the time being.

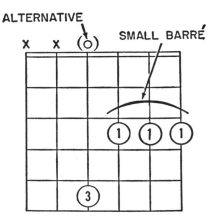

ALTERNATIVE

SMALL BARRÉ

X   X   (○)

**Chord Window
G Minor**

Once again this chord employs the *Small Barré* on the first three strings. Whatever you do, be sure not to sound the 5th and 6th strings in this version of the chord Gm. They are marked X, and they will sound completely wrong if you do sound them.

Now let's try an exercise to get your fingers moving between the chords of D minor. Play this slowly at first, increasing speed as the changes become easier for you.

‖: ¼ Dm / / / | Gm / / / | A7 / / / | Dm / / / :‖

Try this exercise both strumming and string bass style. You can't use the 5th and 6th in the Gm bar, but instead you *can* release your third finger and play the open 4th string as your second bass note.

Minor chords are not only used when playing a piece in a Minor key. Quite frequently a piece that is in a Major will move temporarily into the Minor mood, and then back again to the Major. Like this:

‖: ¼ C / / / | Am / / / | F / / / | G7 / / / :‖

Try playing the four bars above over a few times, experimenting with different rhythmic patterns. This is the sort of chord progression that you can very easily use as an introduction to a song. In this case a song in the Key of C, because the last chord is G7, which leads into C.

Play the introduction in a moderate four to the bar tempo, pausing on the third beat of the G7 to pick up the vocal melody of THE YELLOW ROSE OF TEXAS. The first three notes are your open 3rd string, then the third fret of the 4th string, followed by the second fret of the 4th string. The notes G, F, E – corresponding to the words 'There's a yel-'

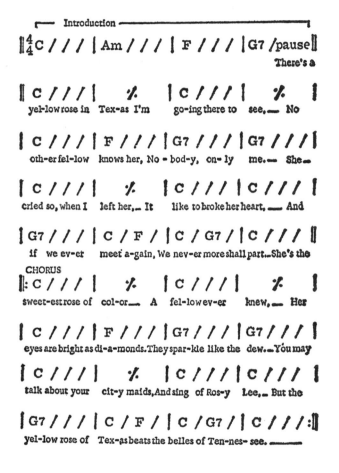

Introductions of the type used above can be used in all keys, but of course the chords have to be changed. Say, for instance, if the song was in G. Then the introduction would be changed to:

‖: ⁴⁄ G / / / | Em / / / | C / / / | D7 / / / :‖

64

Notice that with this type of introduction we *begin* with the tonic chord of the key, and *end* with the dominant 7th. The tonic chord establishes the key in our minds from the outset, then the dominant 7th leads naturally back to the tonic chord. This enables us to start singing in the right place and in the right key.

On the other hand if the introduction were to end on another chord, like this:

‖: $\frac{4}{4}$ G / / / | Em / / / | C / / / | G7 / / / :‖

it is quite probable that we would lose all sense of key and start singing in the wrong one – in this case, probably C instead of G.

Here's another useful introduction chord pattern in the key of C. Notice that once again it ends on the dominant 7th, leading in to the melody of the song.

‖: $\frac{4}{4}$ C / / / | Am / / / | Dm / / / | G7 / / / :‖

Written in G, the same introduction would look like this:

‖: $\frac{4}{4}$ G / / / | Em / / / | Em / / / | D7 / / / :‖

Now let's use this introduction to take us into that old rouser WHEN THE SAINTS GO MARCHING IN. Here again the pick up of the verse comes in on the last two beats of the bar, so you only play two beats on the D7, then pick up the melody notes. The first three notes are open 2nd string, second fret 3rd and open 3rd – corresponding to the words '*I am just*'. The notes B, A, G. Strum a bright four to the bar, and let yourself go with the chorus.

Play these introductions over a few times on their own, and try making up others. You'll find that they will help you to put a song over in a manner that sounds far more 'professional' than just launching into the melody 'cold'.

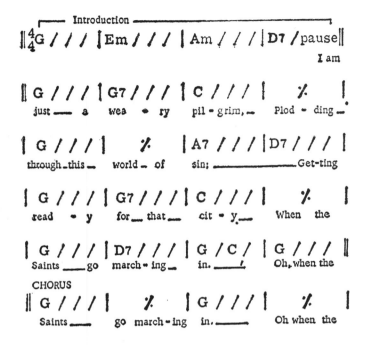

‖ $\frac{4}{4}$ G / / / | Em / / / | Am / / / | D7 / pause ‖

I am

‖ G / / / | G7 / / / | C / / / | ⁄. |

just —— a wea • ry pil - grim, — Plod • ding —

| G / / / | ⁄. | A7 / / / | D7 / / / |

through - this — world - of sin; ————————Get-ting

| G / / / | G7 / / / | C / / / | ⁄. |

read • y for — that — cit • y — When the

| G / / / | D7 / / / | G / C / | G / / / ‖

Saints —— go march • ing — in. —— Oh, when the

CHORUS

‖ G / / / | ⁄. | G / / / | ⁄. |

Saints —— go march - ing in. —— Oh when the

Chapter Nine

DIMINISHED AND AUGMENTED CHORDS

The basic harmonies of most folk songs are pretty simple, and for the purposes of this book I have simplified some of them even further. By now you have no doubt started experimenting with the chords of other songs, and you've probably come across some shapes which you have not yet learned. Two of these will certainly be the diminished and augmented chords. Neither of these are quite as forbidding as they sound, and they are essential to your repertoire of basic chords.

We'll take the diminished first. This is written either Cdim or C°. The basic diminished shape on four strings looks like this:

66

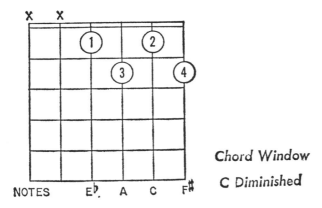

Chord Window

C Diminished

There is something rather special about the diminished chord. It can take its name from any of the notes it contains. Therefore the chord shown above can be called either E♭, A, C or F sharp diminished. Move it up a fret and it becomes E, B♭, C sharp or G diminished. Up another fret (and another semitone) it becomes F, B, D or A♭ diminished. Up one more fret and it becomes F sharp, C, E♭ or A diminished . . . Just a minute! Isn't that where we came in? It is, indeed! Because of this four barrelled system of naming them, there are in fact ONLY THREE DIMINISHED CHORDS, all of which you can play by using the fingering I have given you here and moving up and down on the first three frets.

Here is the process described above shown in chord window form. I have marked the notes of the chord on each string at the bottom of the windows – remember that any of these can be the name of the chord they appear in, in addition to the name given beside the shape.

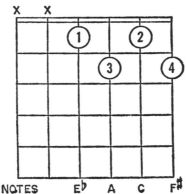

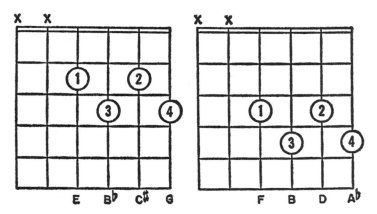

Diminisheds often occur in chord sequences like the exercise given below. Practice this to get the feel of using the chord shape. You can also use this sequence as an introduction to songs in the key of C.

| C / Gdim / | Dm / G7 / | or

| C / Edim / | Dm / G7 / | or C♯ dim
                       or B♭ dim

So much for diminisheds – now what about augmented chords? They couldn't be as easy, could they? Well, as a matter of fact, *they are!* Augmented chords are written either C aug or C+ in symbol notation. The basic four-string augmented shape is like this:

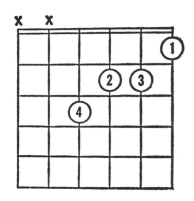

Chord Window
F Augmented

68

Like the diminished, an augmented chord can take its name from any note contained in it. Therefore, the chord shown above can be either F, A or C sharp augmented. Only three? Yes, because the note you are fingering on the 1st string in this shape is a repetition of the one on the 4th string, that is F. There are, in fact, only three notes in the augmented chord.

Now, as you did with the diminished, start moving this chord shape up a fret at a time. Take careful note of what you're doing, referring if necessary to the fingerboard chart at the beginning of this section. You will find that this time you do not start repeating yourself until you get to the fifth fret, with an A on your 1st string. Thus, there are FOUR AUGMENTED CHORDS, all of which you can play by using this chord shape.

Augmented Chord Windows

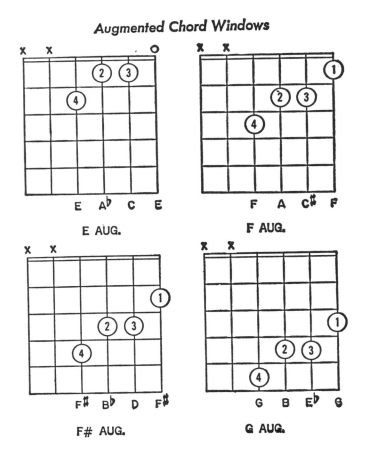

E AUG.

F AUG.

F# AUG.

G AUG.

In a sequence, the augmented chord frequently comes as a bridge between the dominant 7th and the tonic chords, as in this example:

| G7 / G+ / | C / / / |

It is often used at the end of an introduction, like this:

| C / F / | G7 / G+ / |

It will take you time to familiarize yourself with these two types of chord and their names, but you must admit that the principles involved are moderately simple. Once you have mastered augmenteds and diminisheds you should be able to play most pieces in the keys we have studied, with reasonable correctness.

There are still going to be chord symbols in some pieces that you haven't yet learned– for instance minor 7ths, 9ths, major 7ths and 6ths. *At this stage*, THE BEST THING YOU CAN DO WHEN YOU COME ACROSS ONE OF THESE IS TO SUBSTITUTE A CHORD SHAPE YOU ALREADY KNOW. Musically this may not be strictly correct, but if you make the right substitution nobody but a highly trained musician with a very exceptional ear is going to know the difference.

Take minor 7ths first. These are minor chords with the seventh note of the scale added. Therefore, when you come across Em7, or EMin7 written, you can quite safely substitute the Em chord. NOT E MAJOR, PLEASE! because Em7 is based on the minor third interval, which was explained in Chapter Eight, and a major would sound quite wrong.

Now for 9ths. For these you can quite safely substitute the ordinary 7th chord, because a 9th consists of a 7th chord with the ninth note of the scale added. Therefore if you see G9 written, you can play G7.

Major 7th and 6ths we can take together, because in both cases you can substitute the major chord. This is, C6 or C Maj 7 can, for our purposes, equal just plain C. Here again I emphasize that this is *not strictly correct*, but it will sound near enough for the time being.

If you go on to the more advanced studies outlined in Section Four, as I hope you will, you will then learn the correct forms for these chords. But in the meantime, there's no reason, other than sheer pedantry, why you should not substitute as indicated above.

For your last folk song in this section I'm going to give you the chords and lyric of what is probably the finest of our English traditional songs – GREEN-SLEEVES. This has an interesting harmonic structure, switching from major to minor modes and back again several times – AND ending on a chord of D major, despite the fact that it is written in F. The accompaniment is best played in arpeggio style, and with a not too strict beat. The first two notes of the melody are your open 4th string, followed by the same string fingered at the third fret. This gives you the first word *A - las.*

71

Chapter Ten

SUMMARY

Now, for easy reference, here is a summary of all the chords you should have learned to date. They are grouped together in keys, and given once more in window form, with the fullest practical fingering for you.

You've come a long way since you started on Chapter Four. Not in a few days, I know – but you've built up a foundation which should stand you in good stead, whether you decide to stay with simple song accompaniments, or to go on and become a solo instrumentalist.

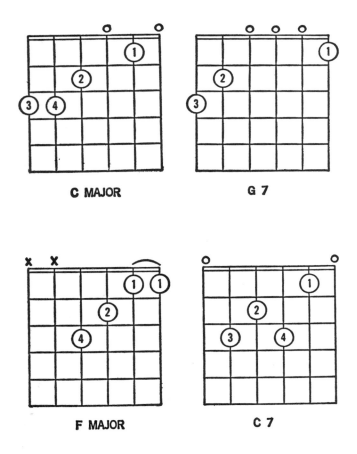

C MAJOR

G 7

F MAJOR

C 7

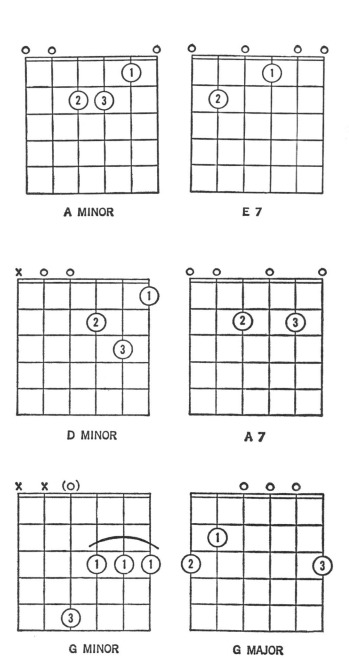

A MINOR

E 7

D MINOR

A 7

G MINOR

G MAJOR

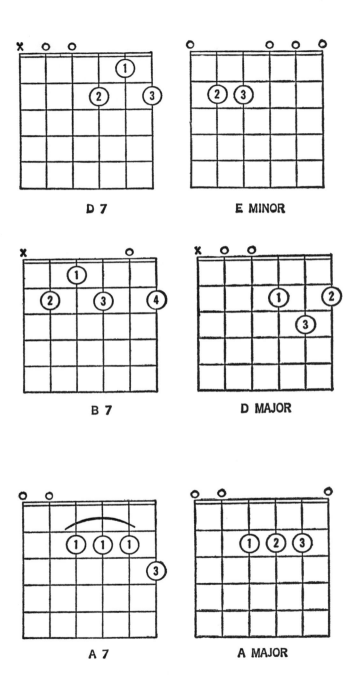

D 7

E MINOR

B 7

D MAJOR

A 7

A MAJOR

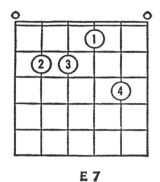

E 7

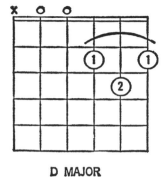

D MAJOR

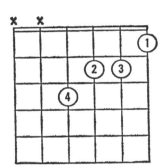

AUGMENTED
SHAPE
A, C# OR F AUG.

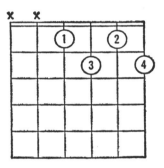

DIMINISHED
SHAPE
Eb, A, C OR F# DIM.

75

Chapter Eleven

ELECTRIC GUITAR

In the days when I started playing, the function of the dance band guitarist was to sit in the rhythm section playing chords all night. Quite often, he was like the proverbial good boy – seen but not heard. Considering the fact that there were probably fives saxes and a similar number of brass instruments in the front line, this is hardly surprising. As for solos – apart from the occasional special effort in the recording or broadcasting studio, these would have been a complete waste of time, as nobody would have heard a note.

I am talking, of course, of the acoustic plectrum guitar. Electric guitar was very much in the experimental stage and viewed with suspicion. There were two important factors about playing dance band guitar at that time – one an advantage, of a kind; and the other, a considerable disadvantage.

The advantage was the fact that you didn't have to read music. The parts consisted entirely of chord symbols; and if you hit a wrong 'un occasionally, it was unlikely that anyone would notice. The *disadvantage*, a Damoclean sword that caused many a brave fellow to desert the guitar for other instruments such as string bass, was the fact that if the bandleader had any cutting down to do, the guitarist was usually the first to get the sack. He was a luxury, and the band could get on quite well without him. I know, because a certain local semi-pro band got along very well without me to such an extent that I spent several liver-lipped years playing trumpet. It is an ironic reversal that today there are many competent brass and reed players who can't get work because of the current guitar vogue.

My lip and patience gave out eventually and I gravitated to the new-fangled electric guitar as the obvious choice. The first thing I discovered was that far from making my playing sound better, amplification seemed to magnify the bad points at the expense of the good ones. No longer mercifully cloaked in inaudibility any wrong notes were now howling bloomers that anyone within a hundred yards could hear. Also, I found that after my years of pounding out an acoustic four in a bar, I was far too heavy handed. There was no longer any need to belt the plectrum down with string breaking force. All you had to do was tickle the strings and let the amplifier take care of the hard labour.

Electric guitar has many of the characteristics of the acoustic instrument, but it also has special problems and advantages of its own. The most important problem that faces an electric guitarist today – the one which may well dictate the future course of the instrument as far as popularity is concerned – is the challenge that faces his inherent musical taste and sense of proportion.

In contrast to the old days when a guitarist had to struggle to make himself heard the modern player of the electric guitar has all the volume he could wish for (and often a great deal more than he needs) at his fingertips. With amplifiers rated anywhere from ten watts up into the hundreds it is possible to make a great deal of *noise* with an electric guitar. But noise is not music.

Somewhere long the line a lot of groups have got hold of the idea that the louder they play the more 'beat' they will have. This is not so. A good performance can be spoiled by playing too loudly, and a bad one can be made even worse. There's absolutely no sense in trying to give your audience shell shock. Play at a reasonable volume, but err rather on the side of quietness – then they may even listen to what you're doing.

ELECTRIC GUITAR STRINGING
If you're playing a solid electric you will almost certainly want to use the type of Light Gauge strings I mentioned in Chapter Three. They make left hand fingering very easy, and help with effects like the Pull and Slur, which I shall explain a little later. If you do use light strings, be particularly careful about your tuning, which can very easily drift off pitch.

For jazz playing on a semi-acoustic I would recommend a rather heavier string, but this again is a matter of taste and the kind of sound you want. Nobody can tell any better than you the sound you hear in your head – and that is what you are out to reproduce.

PICKUPS

Most electric guitars have the adjustable pole piece type of pickup, which enables the balance of individual strings to be altered at will. The 2nd string, for instance, will normally sound louder than the 1st, but with an adjustable pole piece pickup it is a simple matter to iron out this discrepancy. In fact this will already have been done for you with most good instruments, so don't fool around with your pole pieces unless you're absolutely convinced that the balance is wrong.

Most guitars these days have two or more pickups. Two seems quite enough to me – with one placed at the end of the fingerboard and the other close to the bridge. The fingerboard pickup will give a mellow tone and the bridge one a sharp tone. By switching from one to the other you can obtain a complete tonal contrast. More likely, you will use the two together, mixing them through their individual volume controls to obtain the tone you prefer.

That tone depends on the kind of music you wish to play and your own taste. For jazz playing I use a tone that could be described as round, but with an edge – mostly fingerboard pickup, but with a touch of the bridge for sharpness. Some jazz guitarists prefer a plummy, muffled saxophone-like sound, but I like a guitar to sound like a guitar. Aesthetic considerations apart, the plummy sound is hardly likely to cut through the beer drinking chatter of the average Jazz Club crowd.

Rock players normally use a sharp, metallic tone, with the bridge pickup predominating – but here again tastes differ, which is as it should be.

THE VOLUME ADJUSTMENT PROBLEM

A common difficulty for the electric guitarist is the problem presented by a quick change from solo playing to chordal rhythm playing. Clearly if you start pounding out chords at the same volume you were using for the solo the result will be ridiculously over-balanced. But there just isn't time in many instances for you to fiddle around with your volume control knobs. Some makes have got over this problem by installing a switch which modifies the volume of the instrument from solo to rhythm playing at the flick of a finger.

The alternative I have come to prefer, after many years of experimentation, is to use a good Foot Pedal Volume Control. With this you can adjust your volume instantly, within a fraction of a beat. I find the most satisfactory arrangement is to adjust this control at the beginning of a session so that when fully depressed it gives me the maximum solo volume I require. The comping (accompaniment playing) volume can then be finely adjusted at any time to the requirements of the ensemble.

I have found a Foot Pedal Volume Control particularly useful with my Takamine amplified nylon strung guitar, the controls of which are sensibly positioned but practically impossible to adjust in mid-flight.

Apart from Volume Controls there are of course a whole range of Pedal Effects available the Electric guitarist, Fuzz Box, Chorus, Phaser, Flanger etc . . . etc . . . The list increases daily and it may be that you feel you can't live without at least one of them if you're into Rock. Jazz players don't as a rule use any of these effects, other than a touch of reverberation, which is usually built in on good amplifiers.

TREMOLO ARMS

These are mechanical, rather than electronic, gadgets which are standard fitments on many solid guitars. They are a kind of lever attached to a special type of metal bridge which rocks back and forward, changing the tension of the strings and thus causing their pitch to waver up and down. Used tastefully they can produce some interesting and pleasant musical effects.

AMPLIFIERS

As an electric guitarist your amplifier is at least fifty per cent of your equipment. Without a good amplifier the best electric guitar in the world would be a dumb animal. As with your instrument, you would be well advised to buy the best you can afford in an amplifier.

But do take the trouble to define your requirements before buying.

Obviously if you intend to do no more than sit around in the front room and entertain yourself and friends, you have no need of a 100 watt monster. On the other hand, if you intend to play in a group which performs in the average sized hall there will be no point in your relying on one of the 12in by 12in matchboxes that some music stores laughingly call 'amplifiers'.

The practical course, unless you are very wealthy and a genius to boot, lies somewhere in between. Buy a moderately priced amplifier of a reputable make, and buy it from someone who knows what he's talking about and who is in a position to offer you good after-sales service. Don't buy a second-hand amplifier unless the dealer will give you at least a six month guarantee - otherwise you could be buying trouble.

A reasonably good new amplifier which would be suitable for group playing will cost you around £200. On the other hand, when you're starting off you should be quite happy with the kind of small 8 watt Practice amplifier that is available at around £45. A very useful thing about these is the fact that many of them incorporate a Headphone Socket. This will enable you to practise into the small hours without driving the rest of the family and the neighbours crazy.

One drawback of big amplifiers - apart from the price - is their size and weight. After a tiring session mine often feels as if it has been screwed to the floor. That's when I envy my colleague Don, who has a little Polytone amp, which weighs only a few pounds and seems to give just as good sound quality and volume as my own Carlsboro Cobra.

LEFT HAND EFFECTS

One of the major advantages of the electric guitar must be its ability to sustain a note. This makes for a greater smoothness of playing than is possible on the acoustic instrument, and allows for the more efficient use of several special effects. All of these are possible on the acoustic guitar, but they are much more impressive on the electric.

THE PULL

This is obtained by picking a note, then pulling the string sideways, so that the pitch of the string is increased by a semitone. In practice it is better to *push* the string upwards across the fingerboard, rather than using a downward, pulling movement. The reason for this is that on the 1st string a pulling movement may easily result in the string going over the edge of the fingerboard, spoiling the effect completely. After the pull, the string is returned to its normal position, thus lowering its pitch to that of the original note. This means that although the string has been picked only once, three notes have been played. The pull is used a great deal in blues playing, and frequently on the 'blue note' of flattened third of the key, as in the example below:

Another way of using this effect is to pull the string *before* it is picked, and then return it to the normal position. Like this:

THE SLUR

This can be obtained by picking the first of a group of notes, fingering the note with the first finger of the left hand, then with the second and third fingers in quick succession. The second and third notes are not picked, but they will sound quite clearly if you put your fingers down firmly enough, obtaining an effect that sounds like this:

An interesting effect can be obtained by crossing the strings with a slur, as in the example below, which was one of Django Reinhardt's favourite phrases. In this case he used a two note slur – but you can also do the same thing with three notes.

Django's slur looks pretty formidable written down – but in fact it is a trick which once learned you can often use in jazz improvisation without the slightest difficulty, so long as you remember that only the *first* note of each pair should be picked.

The other type of slur is the one in which the same finger is slid up or down the fingerboard to the next note – which is usually a semitone away on the next fret, but can be as much as an octave. That is, as in the following phrase, where the D♭ is touched very briefly before going up to the main note, which is D natural. Here again, this is a favourite type of effect in blues and jazz playing.

Chapter Twelve

BASS GUITAR

Perhaps one of the best things to result from the revolutionary changes brought about by the electrification of the guitar is the general use of the Electric Bass Guitar. This is a four-stringed instrument pitched an octave lower than the standard guitar. Bass guitars are usually Solid, similar to the illustration, but as with other solids the body shape can vary according to the whim of the designer.

Electric Bass Guitar

The bass guitar has largely taken over the role hitherto occupied by the conventional String Bass because it has several advantages over that instrument under modern conditions. With some notable exceptions a lot of string bass players got away with murder in the old days, producing little more than a percussive 'thud' from their instruments and paying little attention to the harmonic correctness of the notes they were fingering.

There can be no such faking on the bass guitar, which produces a clearly audible musical tone and should provide the rock steady rhythmic and harmonic foundation for a group. When the vogue started, many string bass players who thought they were onto an easy number moved over to the bass guitar – only to find that for the first time in their careers they now had to concentrate on playing the right notes.

On the other hand, for a competent guitarist the bass guitar presents an interesting challenge whilst at the same time enabling him to make use of his previously acquired fingerboard knowledge. And don't let anyone imagine that he is taking a step downwards in the musical sense by moving from guitar to bass guitar. In many ways the bass guitarist is the most important player in a group, whether it be rock or jazz. A small jazz group, for instance, can manage without a drummer, but take away the bass player and the whole thing becomes top heavy and begins to fall apart both rhythmically and harmonically.

The four strings are tuned to the same intervals as the *bottom four strings of the guitar* - that is, E, A, D, G. The Bass guitar normally plays a single note bass part, rather than chords, supplying the fundamental harmonic and rhythmic basis to the group. This, coupled with the nature of its tuning, means that any competent guitarist who knows his chords, should be able to find his way around a bass guitar within a very short time and produce a reasonable sounding bass part.

If he wishes, he can do this without even the necessity of reading music in the bass clef, by using the standard guitar symbols. Reduced to its absolute minimum it is possible to produce a correct sounding (if unambitious) bass part, purely on the basis of finding the 'name' note of the chord, then following it with the note on the same fret of the string below. To quote an example - say we have the chord progression in B, as follows:

|| B♭ / / / | E♭ / / / | F7 / / / | B♭ / / / ||

The first note of the bass part would be Bb, which is to be found on the third fret of the 1st string. Now, if we move across, *still on the third fret*, to the 2nd string, the note there is F, which is the fifth of the chord of B♭ major. If a two in a bar bass is required, all we do is play these two notes - the B♭ on the first beat of the bar and the F on the third beat. If a four in a bar is wanted, then we play on each beat, B, F, B♭, F - in that order.

The window below shows you where to find these notes on the bass guitar fingerboard:

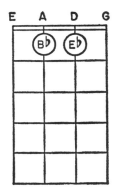

Moving on to the next bar, the chord is E♭. We therefore find E♭, on the first fret of the 2nd string, and next
to it, on the first fret of the 3rd string, B♭. These are the
fundamental notes for this bar and should be played in
the same manner as that described above.

You can find them on the fingerboard, like this:

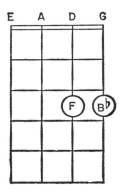

The chord in the next bar is F7. Therefore the next
note is F, which is to be found on the third fret of the
2nd string – and next to it, on the third fret of the 3rd
string is C, which is the fifth of the chord of F7. These
two notes are alternated as in the previous examples.

Find them with the help of this window:

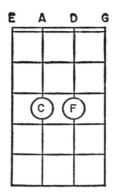

As I suggested earlier, this may not produce a particularly ambitious bass part, but it *is* harmonically correct. On the bass guitar this is important.

With a little bit of thought and practice it is possible to play a more interesting bass part of the walking bass type, like the example below. Here again the progression is based on the name note of the chord and its fifth, but this time the third and sixth notes of the scale are added. Bass guitar parts are normally written in the bass clef, but I have written this example in treble clef notation, so that you can play it on the bass guitar as if you were playing the bottom four strings of a standard guitar.

Take particular notice of the fingering and position markings in this example. (If you are not already familiar with the principle of position playing, this is explained in Chapter Twenty.) The whole piece is based on only one fingering 'pattern', which is played first in the 2nd then in the 4th position. Fingering patterns of this kind are very useful in bass guitar playing, and with a little experiment you should be able to work out any number of them for yourself. They provide a far more efficient method of producing a bass part than leaping up and down the fingerboard willy nilly. Remember that the basis for these patterns is *always* the arpeggio of the chord to be found in the normal guitar part, and you can't go far wrong.

WALKING BASS (12 BAR BLUES)

It is also possible to use the bass guitar for solo
playing, and to turn out some very interesting effects. I
have experimented with bass guitar as a solo jazz
instrument and found it quite fascinating. However,
when improvising solos I occasionally found myself
getting fouled up because of a natural tendency to
think of the strings as the *top four* instead of the bottom
four strings of the guitar. I eventually found a way
round this difficulty by using the 'American tuning',
which is D, G, B, E, the same as the *top* four strings of
the normal guitar. With the aid of this it is possible to

whiz around on a bass guitar at a speed which makes even a first rate string bass player sound like a fumbling amateur. If you want an illustration of what I'm talking about, listen to Wes Montgomery's LP MOVIN' ALONG on the Riverside label.

AMPLIFICATION OF BASS GUITAR
If you are going to get the best out of your bass guitar, you will need an amplifier which is especially constructed for bass response. This means something pretty hefty, with at least a 12in and probably a 15in speaker. Beware of playing a bass guitar through anything smaller – the over-load is liable to wreck a loudspeaker completely.

Chapter Thirteen

JAZZ GUITAR

Over the years the guitar has given me a great deal of pleasure. Especially now that I play predominantly finger style I can sit quite happily on my own tinkling away for hours oblivious to the cares of the world, completely immersed in music. However, I must say that for sheer spontaneous enjoyment there is nothing quite like playing improvised jazz with a good small group..

When a jazz musician plays an improvised chorus he is attempting to perform the miracle of instant composition, and incredibly, if he knows what he's doing the miracle works!

Such a solo is built on the chord progression of the song rather than the melody, so the guitar player has a certain advantage when he comes to jazz. In common with most guitarists I have always found it much easier to remember chord progressions than melodies, which is not surprising, because after some years of playing it is natural to recognize certain chordal relationships.

Any guitarist who wants to play jazz should train himself to do this. He will then be able to develop his solos logically on the basis of the arpeggios and scales thus suggested. Don't misunderstand what I am saying here. A good jazz chorus consists of a great deal more than arpeggios and scales. These should be used as the foundations on which to build a new and interesting melodic line of your own, and added to his basic knowledge of chords and scales the jazz guitarist must have a flair for melodic and rhythmic invention.

Only the geniuses are born with this flair; but fortunately there are ways of developing it through listening and experimentation. Clearly it is no good expecting that you are going to be able to play good jazz improvisations purely by chance. This would be equivalent to sticking you down in the middle of China and expecting you to be able to improvise the language. Jazz is a language; a way of putting over ideas. If you want to play it, you must listen to it habitually, particularly with reference to the guitar; so that you know what has been done and what can be done with our instrument in this field.

If you are really interested in jazz you will have done a lot of listening already. But now you are learning to become something more than a listener. Play your records again, and listen to them from your new viewpoint as a guitarist. Listen dynamically - not passively, as before. Ask yourself questions like; 'How does he do it?' or 'Why did he play that phrase?'

Out of your listening, some phrases will stick in your mind, because they appeal to you personally. Good! This is where style begins. With jazz, as with any other form of self expression - the style is the man. That is to say - your style will be an expression of *your* personality. Try these phrases over on your guitar, working out how they are produced. Some of them will be hard to figure out at first, but keep at it. It is surprising how deeply a phrase worked on in this way can embed itself in your memory; so that later on, almost unconsciously, you will find yourself playing it in the middle of a solo.

Provided you have the ideas - and these will come naturally if you listen enough - the goal you should aim at is *to play any phrase that you can think*, on the guitar. This is of course, an ideal. Very few of us are fortunate enough to reach such a stage of development. In over twenty years of playing I have met less than half a dozen jazz musicians in this calibre - and not one of them has been a guitarist. But remember, there is nothing to be lost by aiming at so high a goal.

How to develop this? I'm afraid that in the last resort it comes down to our old answer: PRACTICE. Practice to the end of becoming completely familiar with your instrument – playing so much that the guitar becomes an extension of your mind. To a much finer degree than that discussed back in Chapter One, this entails establishing a reflex. But, as I said there, it depends entirely on you – on how much work you are prepared to put into attaining mastery of your instrument. You may have wonderful jazz ideas flowing through your mind, but unless you have the technique that is capable of the physical execution of those ideas, you'll be like an elephant trying to fly.

So where do we start? First know your chords. In addition to the run of the mill shapes you've learned already, make yourself familiar with minor and major sevenths, ninths and thirteenths. And know them not just in one position, but all the way up the fingerboard, in all their different inversions. Practise them in arpeggio form in the different positions. Practise scales all the way up the fingerboard, in all keys. Both these scales and arpeggios can be found in the exercise manuals of the type mentioned in Section Four.

Remember one thing; it's no good just playing the exercises over from the music – you've got to learn them if they're going to be any use to you in your playing. So that, for instance, if you are playing a number in B♭, and your hand is in the 5th position, you can quite naturally, without moving your hand, finger a scale passage.

I stress the necessity of learning, rather than just reading and playing mechanically, because when you're actually up there on the stand playing a jazz chorus, there's no time to think coldly about what you're going to play; your ideas must be there at your fingertips, flowing without conscious thought. If you have to think about every note your solo will be stilted and laboured – and it *won't* be jazz.

So what am I saying? Just this: A good jazz guitarist is a GOOD GUITARIST + A FLAIR FOR JAZZ. And there's no way of getting round the requirements of either part of the formula.

PLAYING WITH OTHER INSTRUMENTS

The state of the musical scene today is such that many musicians look upon the guitar as a jazz instrument with some suspicion. Guitar has become a 'commercial' instrument – and jazz musicians are always chary of anything with this label. Another reason for their attitude is the Armageddon situation that I mentioned in the electric guitar chapter. To them, the guitar is an electronic, devouring monster. It's up to you to use your loaf and prove to them – by your playing, *don't* argue – that they're wrong.

In other words, don't start out with your volume up at maximum and try to drown all the other instruments. If you do, you'll only succeed in making yourself look a complete fool, and in confirming their prejudices. Take it easy, and feel your way in. Keep your volume down when you're playing rhythm – and when you come to solo, turn up to a volume that compares with the other, un-amplified instruments.

Like other guitarists, I enjoy almost any kind of guitar playing, even if it isn't particularly brilliant. I just like the sound of the instrument – to such an extent that a reasonably simple phrase played by someone else can leave me trembling with admiration, and wondering if I could possibly ever sound quite as good. With this in mind; although I respect the views of other guitarists, I realize that they are probably just as blind lovers as me. The real kick comes when a musician who plays some other instrument well, tells me he likes the sound.

To you, as a guitarist, the most important man in the jazz group is the pianist. The reason for this is that he is playing the only other chordal instrument in the group; which means that you and he have to come to terms on the chord progression of the numbers you play. Clearly if you have different ideas on the correct chords, the result could be off-putting, to say the least. With this in mind, an indexed address book like the one suggested in Section Two, containing all the jazz progressions you can beg, borrow or steal, can be a great help. At least it will give the pianist an idea of what you're doing, even if his own ideas differ in some cases. He can then either modify his own chords, or suggest others for you to play. And if he *has* any suggestions, for

Pete's sake listen, because most pianists have a theoretical training in harmony that makes us guitarists very much 'Do it yourself' musicians.

Jazz playing offers very little financial reward – you'd be far better off playing pop– but it can give you a great deal of satisfaction if you are fortunate enough to play with a good small group. My own preference is for a quintet lineup of piano, bass, drums and one other instrument, which can be clarinet/sax, vibes, accordion or violin . . . but good jazz violinists are pearls beyond price.

No doubt you're now waiting for the inevitable musical examples– the *How It's Done* written down chorus. I must confess that it was my original intention to perpetrate something of this nature. But on consideration, it seems to me that written 'hot' choruses and books that deliver into your trembling hands 'Five Million Jazz Phrases, as played by Fred Nerk, the Greatest Jazzman of all Time' are, to put it politely, a load of old cod's wallop. Jazz is a living, dynamic form, and you can't get the message from dots on paper. What Fred Nerk played might well have been the greatest, but transcribed to the printed page it loses all the vitality it possessed at that moment of creation when Fred thought of it, or rather, when he played it intuitively. The thing you must do, above all, is LISTEN.

LISTEN to Barney Kessel – who can generate more beat from a single guitar than any ten other people. His solo playing and his comping never fail to inspire both his audience and the musicians with whom he is playing. I have had the privilege of attending three of his Seminars, and if I have learned anything it is that his success has been no accident. Barney has worked harder and thought harder than any other musician I know to get where he is today.

LISTEN to Joe Pass– who has opened up a new world of possibilities for electric guitar jazz with his solo concert performances. Many players have followed his example and started experimenting with the idea of playing the electric guitar with the fingers of the right hand rather than a plectrum. This technique produces a different, less percussive sound, but it offers much satisfaction for those players like myself who have always felt that the guitar should be capable of being a self-contained solo instrument.

LISTEN to Tal Farlow – A soloist whose flow of ideas is nothing short of miraculous, cascades of notes following one another in a dizzying kaleidoscope of sound which makes you wonder how anyone could possibly think that fast. The trick is, of course, that he is such a highly trained and integrated musical unit that he *doesn't need to think in the normally used sense of the word.* Instead he is able to relax and let his instincts take over. This is the ideal situation for a jazz man, but one which very few are able to attain because it requires such a tremendously demanding combination of talent and sheer hard, technical work. Don't ever get the idea that because a master like Farlow makes it look easy what he is doing really is easy.

What you are seeing and hearing is the end product of a lifetime's dedication to the pursuit of excellence.

LISTEN to Jim Hall – a completely different kind of player. Gentle, thoughtful, he never puts a finger wrong; playing a kind of jazz chamber music with a taste and intelligence that make him the thinking man's guitarist.

AND IF YOU WANT TO FIND OUT WHERE A GREAT DEAL OF THIS BEGAN

LISTEN to Django Reinhardt – the incomparable Gipsy guitarist who showed us the way back in the 1930's, whose sheer joy of living comes through with every note, making it impossible to believe that he has been dead for nearly a quarter of a century. If there can be such a thing as an Immortal then Django is surely it.

AND PLAY JAZZ . . .

Chapter Fourteen

SPANISH GUITAR

Having come this far, we can assume that your love affair with the guitar is something more than a passing fancy. It is my hope that something which began as just another hobby has now become an essential part of your life. The guitar is at once a pleasure and a challenge, a delight and a frustration – not only in shape has it female characteristics.

One of the causes of frustration is the plectrum guitar itself – or at least, this was my experience, and I'm sure I'm not alone here. Plectrum guitar is limited in its scope as an unaccompanied solo instrument, because it is not possible to play two or more notes at the same time with a plectrum. The plectrum must move across the strings, striking them one after the other, and while there may be an illusion of simultaneous sound when playing on adjacent strings, like this:

The illusion becomes impossible to maintain when the notes concerned are on widely separated strings – for example in the bar below, where the 6th and 1st strings are used together:

Try this with the plectrum and you'll soon see what I mean. However good your right-hand technique, there is bound to be a perceptible time lag between the low E on the 6th string and the G on the 1st. Now, put your plectrum down and play the same notes by hitting the E with your thumb and plucking the G with the first finger of your right hand, in a kind of pincer movement. This way you can obtain a truly simultaneous sounding of the two strings. This is what the Spanish guitarist does, and this basically is why the Spanish guitar has much greater possibilities.

The Spanish guitar has been likened to a miniature orchestra. Apart from piano, there is no other instrument which is so self contained, or so versatile. And with the guitar, the player has a much more intimate physical part to play in the production of tone than has a pianist. If you want proof of these claims I suggest that you listen to the recordings of Segovia, or our two British greats John Williams and Julian Bream. Or, if you are an un-repentant jazz addict; try Charlie Bird, particularly his trio recordings, where he uses Spanish guitar in conjunction with bass and drums. In these, the guitar effectively takes the place of a piano.

Once having listened, I shall be very surprised if you aren't bitten by the urge to experiment with finger style playing for yourself. Fine! But don't try to do it on your plectrum guitar or you will be very disappointed with the results. Steel strings just don't have the response needed for finger style playing.

The right-hand technique of Spanish finger style playing demands a thicker string of lower tension, made of either nylon or gut. This right hand technique makes use of three fingers and thumb. Think of playing with four plectrums at once and you will begin to understand the reason for the superiority of the Spanish guitar as a self-accompanied instrument.

As far as the right hand is concerned, you have to start again from the beginning; playing exercises to develop this technique. At first you will find that there are many things you could play more easily with a plectrum, but that is only a phase, so resist the temptation.

To find the correct right-hand position, the hand should be allowed to hang relaxed, over the sound hole of the instrument, with the fingers at right angles to the strings. Then the first, second and third fingers are

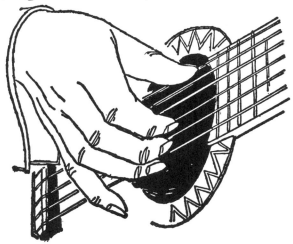

Right Hand Position

placed close to the 3rd, 2nd and 1st strings respectively. From this position only a small movement is required for these fingers to strike the strings. The thumb is held forward from the fingers, pointing along towards the fingerboard, and it moves in the opposite direction to the fingers. When in the correct position, there is no contact, or possibility of interference between the action of fingers and thumb.

I am pre-supposing in this chapter that you already read music. To explore the extensive repertoire of the Spanish guitar, this is essential. If you don't, then it's no use trying to experiment here until you have worked through Section Four.

One of the fascinations of playing finger style is the intricate manner in which pieces are arranged to make use of the special qualities of the instrument. You have only to play through a study by Carcassi or Sor to see how this music is written specifically for the guitar, constructed to exploit the capabilities of both left and right hand in producing the fullest possible musical sound.

In addition to he normal left-hand fingering used in all guitar notation – 1, 2, 3, 4, indicating the fingers of the left hand – in Spanish guitar playing the fingers of the right hand are given, using the abbreviations shown on this page:

1st finger = i (from index)
2nd finger = m (middle)
3rd finger = a (from Anular, or ring)
Thumb = p (from pulgar, or thumb)

Now a simple exercise in C, with fingering, to show you how these right-hand fingers are used. The fingering is marked for the first bar only, and remains the same throughout – thumb, 1st finger, 2nd finger and 3rd finger, in that order.

One of the great composers for the guitar was Ferdinand Sor, who was born in 1778. He wrote a large number of Etudes which are both pleasant to listen to, and very helpful in developing right-hand technique. An example is given below.

Matteo Carcassi was another composer to add greatly to repertoire of the guitar. Here are two short exercises, designed to improve right-hand technique. The first uses a pedal (repeated) note of G at the top, against a moving bass played by the thumb. The second uses a pedal G again, but this time in the middle, on the 3rd string, with a fundamental bass note which rings through the bar – while at the same time a melody is played on the first and second strings. In miniature, this is some indication of the scope of the Spanish guitar from the point of view of orchestration.

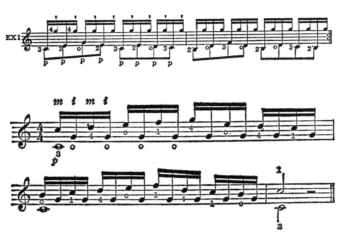

When you have established a reasonable foundation of technique through playing the Classical repertoire you may wish to broaden your horizons by exploring a genre whose richness and variety has only become apparent to me over the past few years. I am speaking of Brazilian Music, which is a fascinating blend of Afro–Jazz rhythms, Modern harmonies and melodic invention.

Including Sambas, Bossa Novas, Waltzes and more exotic Brazilian rhythms, this music is written mainly by guitarists for the guitar, so it is hardly surprising that it sounds so good on the instrument. The works of Luis Bonfa, Antonia Jobim and Baden Powell alone will provide you with sufficient wonderful guitar-oriented music to keep you occupied for several years.

Obviously it isn't possible for me to delve very deeply into the technique of finger style playing in a general book of this nature, but I hope that I may have whetted your appetite sufficiently to make you want to know more. My own book SPANISH GUITAR, also published by Corgi, is designed to provide an introduction to this most rewarding style of playing. You will also find several recommendations for study at the end of Chapter Twenty Five of the present volume.

Chapter Fifteen

FLAMENCO

It has been a standing joke in the guitar world over the last couple of years that there are more flamenco players in London alone than in the whole of Andalusia. An exaggeration, of course, but the fact remains that we have been fortunate enough to have the opportunity of hearing in person a number of great flamenco guitarists, including Carlos Montoya, Sabicas and the younger but no less distinguished Paco Pena. In the hands of these virtuosi flamenco has become almost equal in popularity with the Classical method of playing, and prompted by this tremendous upsurge of interest it has become obvious to me that the brief remarks on the subject of flamenco in the Spanish guitar chapter of the original edition of this book are no longer adequate.

It is the fashion among some classical Spanish guitarists to scoff at the flamenco style, drawing attention to the tonal and technical shortcomings of many of its exponents. Judged by classical standards there may be some justification for this view, but such critics would do well to remember that their own orthodoxy is of a comparatively recent origin, based as it is to a large extent on the work of Segovia over the last sixty years. Formal musicologists raised their hands in horror when the maestro himself first transcribed from the works of Bach and Weiss in order to build the classical repertoire.

However, there is little point in arguing the relative merits of the flamenco and classical styles. The true Flamenco guitar is lighter in build and action than the classical model, two characteristics which facilitate the production of a higher degree of volume at the expense of tone, but essentially the instrument is the same. It seems to me that the basic difference between the two styles lies in the fact that whereas a great deal of the classical repertoire consists of adaptations of works originally composed for other instruments, flamenco is a genuinely primitive art form which has grown naturally out of the characteristics of the guitar itself, and has thus inherited both its limitations and virtues.

The origins of flamenco are obscure, but most authorities agree that they stem largely from the eastern part of the world. Even the untrained ear can detect in the form exotic echoes of Arabian and Hebraic influences. One thing is certain, wherever it originated this music has been adopted and established as their own by the gipsies of Spain. The original role of the guitar in flamenco was – and still remains, some purists would insist – as *part* of that intricate pattern of sights and sounds provided by a troupe of gipsies. The totality of flamenco can only be fully appreciated by witnessing a live performance by such a troupe, and even the sound cannot really be conveyed except possibly through the medium of stereo recording. In adddition to the guitar this sound includes the voices of singers and an incredibly complex pattern of percussive effects provided by the foot-tapping and finger-snapping of the dancers, castanets and hand-clapping rhythms provided by the rest of the ensemble. *A word of warning here*: Carried away by the atmosphere of such a performnce, you may be tempted to join in the hand-clapping. Please *don't!* Unless you have a very good knowledge of the form and a miraculous sense of rhythm it is highly unlikely that your efforts will add anything to the pattern of sound already established, and they will certainly not be appreciated by the performers.

To return to the possibilities of flamenco from the point of view of the lone guitarist, as far as the comparative beginner is concerned the very limitations of the form mentioned above may well prove to be virtues. Consider the fact that almost the entire range of the flamenco repertoire can be performed within the limited key range of E, A, D, C and F, and that a great deal of the time one is likely to be playing no higher on the fingerboard than the third position, and the attractions of this style immediately become apparent. Don't misunderstand me here – I'm *not* suggesting that all flamenco is easy, and that you're going to become a star performer in ten minutes. If you've worked your way through this book so far you know as well as I do that nothing about the guitar is that simple. On the other hand, because flamenco uses the natural qualities of the instrument even a beginner who knows only a few chords should be able, with a certain amount of practice, to produce a series of sounds which bear a recognizable relationship to flamenco.

Perhaps this claim can best be illustrated by suggesting that at this point you pick up your guitar and play the following sequence of chords in the first position: Dm C B♭ A. However you play them, either in arpeggio form or rhythmically, if you have listened to some flamenco there will be something familiar about the sound of this progression.

Now turn your attention to the example below, in which these same chords are written in normal musical notation. The first bar consists of a simple four-string D minor repeated rhythmically, and the second bar of a five-string C major played in the same way. The third bar contains a slightly unusual version of a B♭ major chord with an open E natural on the first string, and the fourth bar begins with a four string A major, moves up to the altered Bb major and returns again to the A major.

RASGUEADOS
The chords above should be played with the index finger of the right hand, striking lightly across towards the treble so that the back and tip of the nail comes into contact with the strings on the down stroke. The upward stroke is merely the reverse of this, returning the finger to its original position. In effect, the first finger plays the role of a plectrum – although you will find it somewhat more difficult to obtain a round, even sound with the finger than is the case with a plectrum,

and a considerable amount of careful practice will be necessary in order to obtain a tone that is not excessively 'scratchy'. This use of the first finger is the basic form of what are known in flamenco as Rasgueados, arpeggios, rolls and rhythmic patterns played with the nails of the right-hand fingers. Rasgueados are largely responsible for the tremendous rhythmic/percussive effects produced by flamenco players and there are so many types that it would be quite impossible to discuss them all in detail here, so I will confine myself to a brief outline of the basic roll.

The basic roll in the rasgueados involves the use of all four fingers of the right hand. Beginning with the right hand in a clenched fist, the fingers are released one at a time with a springing movement, scraping against the palms as they leave it. Commencing with the fourth finger, the nails of the right hand follow each other in quick succession across the strings, producing a continuous chord. An expert flamenco player can keep on repeating this process, producing a solid, continuous roll of sound, but don't break your heart if you can't get the idea in five minutes, because this piece of right-hand technique requires a tremendous amount of practice and muscular control.

Now, back to our four chords, which you will see I have incorporated below in a brief example of the fandanguillo. For the sake of simplicity I have divided this example up into four bar sequences, each of which consists of a flamenco style variation on the original chord progression. These four bar sequences can be repeated according to your own taste, and the piece is brought to a close by a rhythmic repetition of the original four bars.

FANDANGUILLO

Flamenco has many moods and types, but I have selected four of the simpler and more easily playable basic forms for my examples. Each of these four seems to me to have its own particular virtue, either from the point of view of chord progression or rhythmic possibilities.

MALAGUENA: This piece is written in the key of A minor. The chord progression involved is even more simple than that of the fandanguillo, the three chords used being those of E major, A minor and, briefly, F major. The bass notes play a very important part in producing the desired effect in this piece, and they should be played firmly with the right-hand thumb.

MALAGUENA

103

FARRUCA: This is a very popular and rhythmic form of flamenco, and this example will give you an opportunity for further practice of your rasgueados. Pay particular attention to the upward stroke, which can be used quite naturally to play the third chord of each bar. You will note that here again the chord sequence used is extremely simple, consisting of E7, A minor and D minor.

FARRUCA

SOLEARES is one of the grandest and most haunting forms of flamenco. The first sequence of chords should be played with the first finger rasgueado. In the second six bars the bass notes should once again be accented and held with the left hand so as to sound as fully as possible. After this we have a passage in which the melody is played by the thumb against a sustained Tremolo played by the fingers. This type of tremolo is characteristic of a great deal of flamenco playing, and it is produced by alternate plucking of the string concerned – the 1st in this case – by the 3rd, 2nd and 1st fingers, in that order. That is, in Spanish guitar fingering terms *a m i*. As with the rasgueados roll mentioned above, with practice this tremolo can be developed to such an extent that played at speed it becomes a solid, continuous sound. However, at this stage please bear in mind that an even-ness of sound is much more important than speed.

SOLEARES

105

I know that what I have said above will only have served to whet your appetite for flamenco. There are many other aspects of this style which could and should be investigated if you intend to go further, but I'm afraid that for these I must place you in other hands. With this in mind I have examined a number of the publications currently available on the subject of 'How to play Flamenco'. These researches have provided me with no reason to alter my original opinion that by far the most comprehensive and understandable work on the subject remains *Flamenco Guitar* by Ivor Mairants.

Chapter Sixteen

USING A TAPE RECORDER

Tape recorders are fascinating toys. People spend thousands of pounds on them each week, and most of them are used to no more useful purpose than recording Uncle Fred barking like a dog, or recording Rover, who makes noises like Uncle Fred. YOU, on the other hand, have a cast iron excuse for buying a tape recorder – because you can make real, practical use of it.

Merely from the routine practice point of view, you will find a tape recorder most useful. Switch it on at the beginning of a practice session, making sure that your recording volume is within reasonable limits, then forget about it. The resultant tape can then be played back at your leisure and listened to with a critical ear. They'll all be there, the clangers, the buzzes and the mumbled curses. The first time or two your ego may droop pretty badly, but your eyes, or rather your ears, will be opened. Remember that, for better or for worse, this is *your* playing – the brilliant passages where you sound just like Eric Clapton, and the rough ones where you sound like nothing on earth – *they're all yours.*

Incidentally, don't play this tape to anyone else – you're liable to lose friends that way. These practice sessions should be as personal and private to you as your diary or toothbrush. If you want to make a special tape to amaze your friends, that's another matter altogether which we'll discuss later on in this chapter.

From these taped practice sessions you can learn about the three Ts: Tone, Timing and Technique. The three are closely tied together, of course, but first let's take them separately.

TONE

Bearing in mind the remarks made elsewhere on this subject, what sort of a noise are you producing from your instrument? Is it full and pleasing to the ear, or is it scratchy and unpleasant? When I say *full*, I don't mean LOUD. Is every note being given its full value, and is it being produced with a minimum of clicks and buzzes? If you are using an amplified guitar, your tone can vary from a plummy, Chuck Wayne type tone, right up to a screaming Wild Dog, beat effect. Only *you* know what you're aiming at – and the tape recorder will show you just how near you are getting to it.

The electric guitar is a difficult instrument to record, as any sound expert will tell you, so don't just stick the microphone of the recorder in front of your amplifier and expect it to come out right. The best way to record is to plug the guitar directly into the recorder. That way you will get a much truer picture of the sound your pickups are producing. Of course, if you're playing an acoustic guitar then you'll have to use the microphone. In that case the microphone should be placed within a couple of feet of the soundhole rather than somewhere on the other side of the room.

To return to the subject of Tone.

Don't forget about your plectrum. If it's too thick, your tone will be 'tubby' – if too thin, it will be clicky and tinny. Aim somewhere in between. Are your UP and DOWN strokes equal in tone? They should be, if you're holding the plectrum correctly – if you're not, you'll be able to tell by the thinness of the UP stroke notes. Are you hitting the strings with the correct force? Or are you producing rattles and buzzes, particularly on chords? What is the condition of your strings? If the coverings are beginning to wear, they may become frayed and cause buzzing.

TIME

Do you finish each exercise or solo at the same speed as you started? And is this tempo maintained throughout? Beware of the tendency to play parts which fall easily under the fingers more quickly, slackening off again when you come across a more complicated passage. This is incorrect – as I have remarked elsewhere, the ability to keep a steady tempo is one of the most important requirements of a guitarist. Any piece you play – study, exercise or solo, should not be commenced at a tempo any faster than that at which you are able to play its most difficult passage with comfort.

TECHNIQUE

Are you hitting the right notes at the right time, and in the right order? The most logical left-hand fingering is probably indicated on the copy – *take notice of it*. If you're jumping up and down the fingerboard, snatching for notes, this will be evident in the sound you produce. Play in the positions indicated, and use the fingers indicated. You'll find it much easier in the long run, and much more effective. Do your changes in chordal passages sound smooth? If not, go back and practise changing the chord shapes over and over again. Then re-record the passage and see how it sounds.

Above all things – remember what Andres Segovia has said: 'Never forgive yourself one mistake!' In other words – don't ignore faults, CORRECT THEM. The tape recorder can help you to do this. It can be your friend and severest critic, because it cannot lie or flatter.

SELF ACCOMPANIMENT

So far we have only talked about recording your practice and replaying the results for later evaluation, but there is a great deal more that you can do with a tape recorder.

For a start you can record chordal accompaniments to back your own single string solo playing. This is a tremendous help for practising improvisation because it allows you to experiment without any inhibitions, trying out the wildest of ideas in the confidence that even if they sound awful they will remain a confidential secret between you and your recorder.

As I said earlier, this is the way it should be. Nobody else appreciates, or wants to know the struggles you have to attain the kind of sound you're looking for. When you think you've got it right play to other people by all means, but don't let anyone else hear your preliminary fumblings.

Barney Kessel has a very wise saying which sums this up 'Practise your weaknesses in private – Exhibit your strengths in public.' In other words, you should not attempt to play anything to an audience until you're 200% sure of it.

A very useful aid to the kind of practice mentioned above is the Phillips D6550, which is a small, lightweight amplifier with a built in tape recorder. On ordinary tape recorders you will sometimes find that although your accompaniment was in perfect tune when you recorded it, on playback it comes out unpleasantly sharp, or more likely flat, so that you have to adjust the tuning of your guitar if you are to play along with it.

The big advantage offered by the Phillips is that it incorporates a Tape Speed control which can be used on Playback to adjust the tuning of the pre-recorded accompaniment and bring it into line with your 'live' guitar. Add to this the fact that it has three different input sockets, plus an output for headphones and that's quite a package for around £120.

Suppose, for instance that you have a drum machine, you can plug this into one of the other inputs when you're recording your accompaniment. Then when you come to play back and add your 'live' guitar part, instead of a duet you will have a trio. Apart from sounding fuller, this has the advantage of holding a rock steady rhythm because of the discipline provided by the electronic 'drummer'. I've used this gimmick a couple of times to play to a small audience, and most people are rather impressed that one player can make such a sound with what is apparently a single guitar.

Just a word of warning, if you intend to try the same sort of routine – Record the open strings of your instrument at the beginning of your recording session. Then before you begin to perform check the tuning of those recorded open strings with your guitar, making any necessary adjustment on the Playback Speed of the recorder – *not on your guitar.*

MULTIPLE TRACK RECORDING

The kind of thing mentioned above is quite elementary compared with the elaborate recording techniques available today. The simplest of these is performed by another little gadget I acquired some time ago, called a TENSAI RHYTHM BOX which is a small tape recorder incorporating both a drum machine and an After Recording system.

With this machine I can record the rhythm guitar part and drums as mentioned above on the Phillips machine. But with the After Recording facility the process can be carried a stage further, because it enables me to play back the guitar and drums and record a solo guitar part at the same time, so that I end up with the Dan Morgan 'trio' on the finished tape.

Moving a step further along from the above, both financially and musically, if you really want to get into the recording business there are quite a few different multiple track recording decks on the market such as the Fostex and Tascam which will enable you to record up to 6 different parts onto the same tape. The price of this type of recorder starts around £300 and the sky's the limit. With this kind of equipment a small group can produce a reasonable demo tape, which could be useful. As you probably know already, recording studio time comes pretty expensive, so the investment in a multi track deck could well be worthwhile.

Chapter Seventeen

MEET THE FAMILY

With the guitar in its different forms so much a part of our contemporary musical life it is difficult to believe that only a few decades ago it was considered something of a poor relation in comparison with other, more popular fretted instruments. Ironically, there are today definite signs that the dominance of the guitar is, in its turn, producing a revival of interest in the other fretted instruments. Attics and second-hand shops are gradually disgorging half-forgotten instruments which most people find difficult to name, let alone play.

BANJO
The best known fretted instrument other than the guitar must surely be the frying-pan shaped banjo. In its commonest form this is a five-stringed instrument with a round body which is covered by a stretched vellum like the head of a drum, and a long neck.

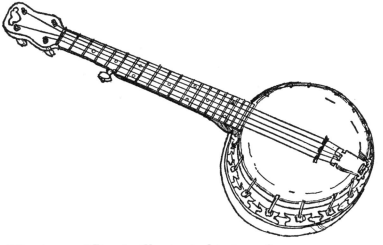

The type of Banjo illustrated is tuned:

and is played with the fingers of the right hand. As you will see from the musical notation above, the G of the 5th string is *not*, as we might expect from our experience with the guitar, lower in pitch than the 4th, but is in fact an octave higher than the 3rd. This small string, which begins at the fifth fret rather than the nut, is a *chanterelle*. Not normally fingered with the left hand, it is played as an open string, producing a singing, high-pitched G.

The tenor-banjo is a four-stringed instrument, tuned:

and played with a plectrum. This was the instrument which replaced the more modest toned un-amplified plectrum guitar in the early days of jazz. Anyone who

111

has any doubts about the reason for this takeover by the banjo need only listen to one of our present-day trad jazz bands to hear how the percussive, piercing tone of the banjo is capable of dominating a rhythm section and cutting through the sound of a loud-blowing ensemble of front-line instruments.

The bluegrass (folk) style of banjo playing has attained considerable popularity over the last few years, having been brought into prominence by the performances of such players as Pete Seeger and Earl Scruggs. This attractive manner of playing is similar to the country and western 'duo style' of guitar used by Chet Atkins and others. It is played with the fingers of the right hand on a banjo which has an extra-long neck with three more frets than the standard model, and is tuned:

Apart from obvious extensions such as the bass – or more correctly, the cello-banjo, and the contra-bass banjo, which is the banjo equivalent of the double bass, there are a large number of variations which although retaining the same basic shape vary considerably in length of neck, number of strings and tuning. These include the banjolin, which has four single, or eight 'double' strings; the mandolin-banjo, which is virtually a mandolin with a banjo-shaped body as the name implies, and the four-stringed ukulele-banjo, which was popularized by such well-known performers as George Formby and Tessie O'Shea.

MANDOLIN
This is an eight-stringed instrument, with four sets of 'double' strings which are tuned:

like the violin, but is played with a plectrum. The mandolin is a solo instrument, rather than a chordal or rhythmic one like the guitar or banjo. It has a mellow, but penetrating tone, and perhaps the most characteristic feature of its sound is the tremolo, the production of which is made easier by the unison-tuned 'double' stringing.

The traditional Neapolitan mandolin as illustrated has a bowl-shaped back, although many modern American instruments have a flat back, or a cello top and back with F-holes, rather than a round soundhole.

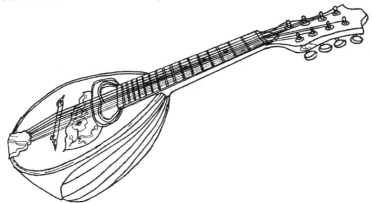

The older type of Italian mandolin, the Milanese, had a similar body shape to the Neapolitan, but was strung with *six single* strings of gut and played with a swan quill or piece of buffalo horn.

LUTE

This ancient instrument has recently found a new lease of life, in large measure due to its concert use by Julian Bream. Although we tend to look upon the lute as a typically Old English instrument of the sixteenth and seventeenth centuries, it was popular throughout Europe and many countries have their own form with different stringings and tunings. The lute is played with the fingers of the right hand, and the most commonly used tuning nowadays is:

It will easily be deduced from this that a Spanish guitar player may, if he is not averse to cheating a little, make things considerably easier for himself by tuning the 3rd string up a semitone to G.

The lute illustrated above is of the tradional, broken-neck shape. Very slightly built of multiple veneers, this instrument has a delicate, sharp tone, less full-bodied

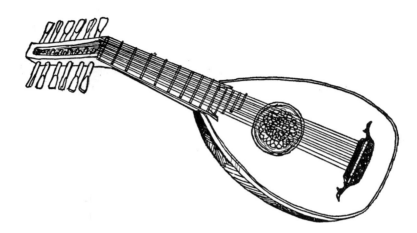

than that of the guitar. It has six sets of 'double' strings and the traditional gut frets, although I am told that the more legitimate number of strings is now considered to be ten – the 1st and 2nd strings single and the rest 'doubled'. Either method would seem to be more sensible than the stringing on a modern German instrument which I examined recently. This had six single strings and was really little more than a pear-shaped guitar. There is surely no point in abandoning one's first love for such an alternative.

UKULELE

This is a small instrument which looks very much like a miniature four-stringed guitar. The etymology of its name is of some interest, being derived from the Hawaiian words *Uku* – meaning flea, and *Lele* – from the verb to dance. Ukulele therefore = Dancing Flea. Mainly used as a rhythm instrument the ukulele had a considerable vogue in the twenties and thirties both as a vocal accompaniment and in Hawaiian ensembles.

The Ukulele originated in the Hawaiian Islands and its traditional tuning is:

although there are variations on this such as the

soprano and bass tunings. The instrument lacks the
sustaining power and sonority of the guitar, but its
mellow tone, the ease with which simple chord shapes
can be formed when dealing with only four strings, its
comparative cheapness and its extreme portability –
vide the extraordinary Tiny Tim's carrier-bag routine –
make it an attractive little instrument which changing
fashions in popular music may yet return to prominence.

BALALAIKA
This is a traditional Russian instrument, with a thin
neck and an oddly-shaped triangular body. The name
is derived from the Russian Laika – box, and Bala –
chatter. Thus Balalaika = Chatterbox, which is aptly
descriptive of the sound of the instrument. The Balalaika has three strings, the 1st tuned to A and the 2nd
and 3rd to E in unison, at the same pitch as the Spanish
guitar 1st string. Although originally played with the
fingers of the right hand, of latter years there has
arisen a vogue for the use of a plectrum, and the
stringing has in some cases been 'doubled'. Like the
banjo, balalaikas come in all sizes from the piccolo to
the contra-bass.

SITAR

This traditional Indian instrument has received a great deal of publicity over the past few years, although I feel that this was probably stimulated more by the Beatles' adventures in the land of Transcendental Meditation than by any genuine musical interest. Those of us who have been privileged to hear the astonishing sitar improvisations of Ravi Shankar cannot fail to admire the technique and artistry involved, but from a playing point of view it is as well to remember that musically speaking the sitar exists in a different world from the one in which we live.

Indian music is based on concepts which are so alien to our own that it cannot even be written down in what is to us normal musical notation. Unless one's ear is attuned to the strange intervals involved – and this must be very rare among Westerners – it is not possible for us even to begin to play the kind of music for which the sitar has been designed. On the other hand, it seems to me that to attempt to adapt the sitar to play *our* kind of music – while it may have a certain novelty value – can hardly be considered a musical exercise of sufficient seriousness to warrant the high cost of buying one of these magnificent instruments. However, if you are *really* serious and sufficiently dedicated, by all means follow the example of a young cellist friend of mine, who has found himself an Indian teacher with whom he is studying the sitar.

HAWAIIAN GUITAR

I cannot possibly conclude this brief outline without remedying one glaring and unforgivable omission on my part in the original edition of *Guitar* – namely the Hawaiian guitar. Originating as its name implies in the Hawaiian Islands, this instrument is played in a unique position, lying flat on the lap. The reason for this is the fact that the left hand, instead of fingering in the normal manner, stops the strings with a bar of metal called a steel. (From which we get the misnomer Hawaiian steel guitar, which suggests a guitar made of metal.) The strings do not come into contact with the frets during the playing of the Hawaiian guitar, and these are usually inlaid rather than raised, serving only as a position guide on the fingerboard. Because of

116

this a perfect *glissando* can be played on the Hawaiian guitar – a feat which is impossible on any other fretted instrument for obvious reasons. (To look on the dark side, it is also possible to play the Hawaiian guitar excruciatingly out-of-tune.)

The Hawaiian guitar is played by the thumb and fingers of the right hand in a manner similar to Spanish finger style, but often with the assistance of metal or tortoiseshell thumb and finger picks. It is mainly a solo instrument, but chords can be played. There are many different tunings, among which one of the most popular is the A7. This gives a chord of A7 when played across the open strings, and of course a chromatic succession of 7th chords as the steel is placed on the strings and moved up the fingerboard. My own taste is for an E7 tuning, because this is closer to normal Guitar tuning – the only differences being that the 5th string is tuned to B and the 3rd to G sharp.

The singing tone of the Hawaiian guitar is unique and extremely attractive. Some twenty years ago it was used as the lead instrument in such ensembles as the Felix Mendelsohn Hawaiian Serenaders and A. P. Sharpe's Honolulu Hawaiians, but apart from the recordings of Wout Steenhuis and the playing of a handful of others it is seldom heard today. The Hawaiian guitar benefits considerably from amplification – the model illustrated above is a modern electric version – and I cannot help thinking that it is an instrument which has not yet been exploited to the full from the point of view of popularity.

The most pleasant aspect of preparing this brief review of the fretted instrument family has been the time I spent with that well-known teacher and performer Geoff Sisley, who has assisted me in my researches into aspects of fretted genealogy hitherto unfamiliar to a mere guitar player. I am greatly indebted to Geoff, who is a veritable mine of information and anecdote about every conceivable aspect of this enormous field. He is also, by the way, a prolific arranger and composer of music for the Spanish guitar, having published collections such as THE ROMANTIC GUITAR (Chappell & Co) FAMOUS MELODIES ARRANGED FOR THE SPANISH GUITAR (Ricordi) THE DEEP SOUTH GUITAR (Chappell & Co) and many others.

Section Four

Chapter Eighteen
LET'S LEARN TO READ

Chordal accompaniments are only part of the story. Sooner or later the budding guitarist is going to play proudly through a chord progression, only to be rudely jarred by a boorish friend who says: 'Yes, that's all very fine, but what about playing a tune we can recognize!'

If you have a good singing voice this difficulty may never be encountered, but if – like mine – your vocal ability is something less than sparkling, you're up the creek. Or rather, you've come to a junction in the stream of your musical career at which you have to make a choice. Either you're going to paddle along gently, playing chord accompaniments for other people (whose voices are probably no better than yours) OR you're going to take the other fork, which leads right into the mainstream of guitar playing, and learn to become a solo guitarist.

If you make the first choice, then you get along indefinitely using chord symbols – but if you want to become a soloist, then you may as well admit here and now that you've got to start learning to read music. At this point in a class some sharp cookie usually bobs up and mentions either Django Reinhardt or Wes Montgomery, or both. It has always been part of the Django legend that he couldn't read music, although I have recently heard this refuted most indignantly by a musician who knew him. He insisted that the idea was ridiculous because (*a*) Django was a violinist before he ever played the guitar, which indicates at least some legitimate training, and (*b*) that his technical ability would have been quite impossible to attain without some theoretical knowledge in the matter of scales and arpeggios. The same kind of story is told about Wes Montgomery, but as he, like Django, is unfortunately no longer with us, there doesn't seem to be any satisfactory way of settling the argument.

In any case it wouldn't prove a thing, because unless you're in *their* genius class – in which case you probably don't need lessons from me or anybody else – you'll find it a great help to be able to read. Without a really exceptional ear, which is about a one in a million chance, it's impossible to make any real progress as a guitarist unless you have a certain amount of musical theory. After all – would you stand much chance of reading a book, if you didn't know the letters of the alphabet? The only consolation is that learning to read music is far easier than learning the alphabet.

The guitarist's problem is to relate what is written down in musical notation to his fingerboard and the movement of his fingers. It's a slow, fumbling process at first, but with practice your fluency will increase. It won't happen overnight – but sooner or later you will find new dimensions being added to your musical awareness, as you explore first the music written for solo guitar, then start experimenting with piano and violin parts. I recommend starting first with music arranged expressly for the guitar, because this usually has such aids as fingering and position guides. With music written for other instruments it is necessary to carry out your own adaptation to make it playable on the guitar. This entails such tasks as changing chord inversions and transposing octaves to make the piece fall under your fingers, so that your left hand is not forced to scramble up and down the finger-board like a demented spider.

I said above that learning to read music is far easier than learning the alphabet, and now I'll prove it. The musical alphabet consists of only seven letters: A B C D E F G, which repeat themselves: G A B C . . . etc. All sorts of weird and wonderful systems have been invented to enable you to play the guitar without reading music, but apart from the 'window' system of chord diagrams, the uses of which you have already seen, they are all far more trouble than they're worth, and nowhere near as efficient as standard musical notation. The use of the staff with its five lines and four spaces, has been developed over centuries as the best way of communicating musical sounds on paper – so it should be good enough for you and me.

Lines

Spaces

The Notes of the Treble Clef

It is essential from the very outset that you should think of the notes on the staff as actual sounds on the guitar, and not as something vague and theoretical. Our final aim is to establish a reflex - a natural movement of the hands on the instrument in response to the stimulus of the note on paper. This probably sounds a bit high falutin, but all it amounts to is something far less complicated than learning to touch type. It's as easy as learning to ride a bike- and you can learn it in a similar way, by keeping on trying until you stop falling off. One advantage with the guitar is that bruises don't show.

Music for the guitar is written in the treble clef, indicated by this sign: &

The guitar, in fact, sounds an octave lower than it is written. This is done to make the music easier to read, and is thus a mere matter of convenience that need not concern us at this point.

The open strings of the guitar, as you already know, are tuned E A D G B E. When written on the treble clef staff, they look like this:

You will notice that the open string sounds of the 4th, 5th and 6th strings are written beneath the normal lines of the staff. The extra lines used for this purpose are known as leger lines, and are used for notes either below, or above the range of the staff.

121

Any note on the staff may be preceded by either a sharp: or a flat: - which means that it is either played a semitone higher, or a semitone lower. In guitar language this means either one fret higher, or one fret lower. For example, let's take the C on the first fret of the second string:

Now, if this note were written:

you would move your fingering up to the *second* fret. If, on the other hand it were written:

you would move your finger down one fret, which in this case means to play the open 2nd string, B - which is the equivalent of Cb because there is only a semitone between B and C in the scale.

All music is divided up into bars, like this:

And the number of beats in the bar is determined by a time signature. Therefore, 3/4 is, three in a bar, 4/4, four in a bar; 2/4, two in a bar, and so on . . .

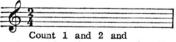

The notes we have been using so far are semibreves: **O** which have a time value of 4 beats, and should be counted 1, 2, 3, 4. Thus we play the open strings of the guitar in semibreves:

Next, with half the time value of a semibreve, comes the minim: ♩. This has a time value of 2 beats, and should be counted 1, 2. Now play the open strings in minims:

Count   1-2 1-2   1-2 1-2   etc.

Half the time value of the minim gives us one beat, which is the crotchet: ♩ . There are therefore four crotchets in a bar of 4/4 time, like this:

Count   1 2 3 4   1 2 3 4   etc.

Halving the time again, we have the quaver: which has a value of half a beat, and can be counted one and, two and, three and, four and. There are therefore eight quavers to a bar of 4/4, like this:

Count   1 & 2 & 3 & 4 &   etc.

The semiquaver, as its name implies, is half a quaver and it looks like this: . There are therefore sixteen semiquavers to a bar of 4/4 - like this:

Count   1 & 2 & 3 & 4 &   etc.

To correspond with each of these notes there is a rest, which indicates a period of silence.

**Rests
with Corresponding Note Values**

I don't expect you to take in all the information in this chapter at once, but I've set it all down here at the beginning of the section so that you have it for reference when you need it. *Do*, however, play over the examples above on your guitar. When you are confident that you can do this without fumbling, turn to the next chapter.

Chapter Nineteen

THE KEY OF C MAJOR

PRACTICE

Now that we are on the road to *real* guitar playing, this seems a good time to have a word about the idea of PRACTICE in general. *Practice* seems to be a dirty word among many beginners – they resent it as a chore to be got over as soon as possible, so that they can get down to the more interesting and glamorous part of guitar playing. If you sincerely want to become a good guitarist, now's the point at which you should indulge in a bit of self analysis. Have you got that 'Get away with as little as possible' attitude about practice yourself? If so, this is the time to get rid of it.

For a starter, ask yourself why you want to play the guitar. I *have* heard people say that they want to do it just for the money. That seems to me like applying for a professorship before you've passed your GCE. I might also add that I've been playing the guitar for over twenty years, and I'm still about nine hundred and ninety nine thousand away from making my first million – so there must be easier ways of making money. A much better reason to me by a student once was: 'If you can play the guitar you'll have a lot of friends, and you'll never be lonely.' But I think the best and only true reason is the one mentioned in Chapter One – and if you don't remember what *that* is, you'd better go back and have a look right now.

If you have the right attitude of mind, playing the guitar is a pleasure – *and practice is guitar playing.* So how can it be hard work? The more you practise, the more proficient you will become, and as your command of the instrument increases, you will get more and more pleasure out of using your ability. Sometimes you'll find that the real effort comes in putting the instrument down and forcing yourself to get on with the more mundane things like eating and making a living.

That isn't to say that there won't be times when you just don't feel like playing; when you've either over-exerted your resources, or you're just feeling generally browned off and can't be bothered to do *anything.* If you are really tired, all right – go out and do something else. The change will do you good. But if you're just bored with life, why not try getting down to some real practice? Chances are that you'll get so interested in what you're doing that you'll forget how fed up you were when you started. There's nothing quite so satisfying as doing something creative, and doing it well.

THE DIATONIC SCALE

Our first exercise is the diatonic scale, which is simply a scale with one note on each line and each space of the staff. This scale starts on your open 6th string and ends on the third fret of your 1st string. I have indicated the finger, string and fret for each note – follow them carefully.

Play this scale slowly, using down strokes of the plectrum, making each note sound its full value and repeating to yourself the name of each note as you play it – E, F, G, etc. Don't let yourself get away with any buzzes and clicks. By now you should know how to put your fingers down correctly and eliminate these.

Now here is the same scale, but going downward.

Again play this scale slowly, repeating to yourself the name of each note as you play it and following the fingering directions carefully.

Now take a look at this succession of notes:

Does it suggest anything to you? It is in fact, the C major chord which you learned earlier, and its notes are, from the bottom up: G, C, E, G, C, E. When the chord is to be played as a whole, as when strumming, the notes are piled on top of each other, like this:

Looks rather fearsome, doesn't it? But don't worry, I only did it to illustrate the point of how chords are written on the staff. Just think of it as the old six-string C major.

Now two more bars:

Familiar? Remember we talked about the string bass style in Section Two? Well, this is the chord of C written in that style, with single bass notes on the first and third beats of the bar and the chord on the second and

126

fourth. You have probably played these two bars many times already, but now play them and relate them to their shape on paper.

Now two more bars that should – dare I say it? – strike a chord.

Playing again in the string bass style, this is the chord of G7. Now, by putting these two chords together and adding a few more bass notes, I'm going to give you a simple duo style solo to play. Duo style is the name given to this kind of self accompanied playing, which has a single note melody on the bass strings, alternating with chords on the higher strings. This is also the kind of thing you might play as an accompaniment, in line with my remarks about interesting accompaniments in Section Two. You will notice that some of the notes have their tails pointing upwards in the normal manner and some have tails which point DOWNWARDS. This device is used to distinguish the two parts – the melody and the accompaniment. The notes with their tails downwards are the bass string melody, of course.

The eight bars are enclosed between repeat signs:

||:‖:||

The device of a 1st and 2nd time bar is also used here. This is used to do away with the need of writing out the whole 16 bars of the solo. The first time through you should play up to the double bar, then go back to the beginning and repeat. BUT on this second playing, you *miss out* the two bars enclosed by the bracket above and labelled 1st – going straight on to the two bars marked 2nd. Like this:

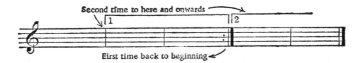

I have written another little piece in duo style – this time in 3/4 waltz tempo. Here again we're using only the chords of C and G7, but this time the melody has moved up to the 2nd, 3rd and 4th strings. You have to familiarize yourself with the notes in the first position, and the most interesting way to do this is by actually playing pieces that use these notes. In this waltz you will notice that there are a number of notes which are followed by dots, like this: ♩. . These are known as dotted notes, and the presence of the dot increases their time value by *half*. That is, a dotted minim is equal to *three* beats, a dotted crotchet to one and half beats and so on.

If you're a jazz or rock fan, you may not consider that this duo style type of playing is particularly 'with it'. Maybe not, but it's a good way of getting to know the fingerboard and at the same time making a reasonably pleasant sound.

Take your time with these two pieces, paying attention to the fingering where it is marked – and try to relate the notes on the paper to what your fingers are doing.

TULIP WALTZ

Now that you've played a couple of elementary tunes, let's go back and have a look at the scale of C in the first position.

Play this, slowly at first, increasing speed as you gain in confidence. Here again, it is essential that you should think about the notes on the paper and relate them to the patterns made by your fingers on the fingerboard. You will derive more benefit from this type of practice at this stage if you deliberately *don't* attempt to memorize the exercises, but *read* them afresh each time you play them.

Now, if you're sure of the scale of C in the first position, here's a little exercise based on it. Try this over, using the fingering indicated – slowly at first, remember . . .

How did that go? All right? Maybe I'm odd, but I quite enjoy playing that type of exercise, because it has a logical pattern of sound and fingering. I hope you feel the same way, because such exercises can be invaluable in developing both left- and right-hand techniques.

Now let's try another little piece in C. I've written this one as a single note melody, with the chord symbols underneath. You will notice that at certain points I have inserted an instruction: HOLD CHORD. This is where the melody is based on the arpeggio of the

129

actual chord shape, and at these times you should hold your left-hand fingers down and let the notes of the chord ring. This way you will obtain a much fuller effect than just playing single notes as written.

JULY EVENING

Slowly

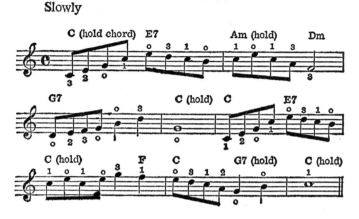

Take in A/W p154

Chapter Twenty

THE KEY OF F MAJOR

In our study of chord symbols in Section Two we explored the keys of C, G, D and A. C is the open key, with no accidentals, and the other three are all sharp keys. I did this for reasons of simplicity, because the sharp keys are the easier, more natural ones for the guitar. In this section I propose to go a certain way in the opposite direction – through the flat keys.

Having said this, I should explain to you what is meant by a sharp, or a flat key. In Chapter Nineteen all the pieces and exercises were written in C, the open key, which is identified by this key signature:

Try this scale:

It doesn't sound quite right, does it? and the note which doesn't fit is the open B on the 2nd string.

Now try the same scale, but with the B flattened, and played on the third fret of the 3rd string, instead of the open 2nd.

This is the true scale of F major – which contains a B♭ at its seventh degree. To make matters easier, instead of marking this B♭ every time it appears as an Accidental, the fact that it is flattened is indicated in the key signature thus:

Signature
Key:
F

This tells us at the outset that we are in the key of F, and at the same time reminds us that all the B's in this key are flattened.

Now let's try an exercise like the one we had in Chapter Nineteen, but putting it this time in the key of F. As we are using F as our starting note, we can start down on the first fret of the 6th string and go up two whole octaves to the F on the first fret of the 1st string, like this:

The principal chords in the key of F are F, C7 and B♭, and now is the time for you to learn them, if you aren't familiar with them already. This time I have introduced the *Great Barré*, with the first finger going right across the fingerboard and holding down the 1st, 2nd and 6th strings in the F chord; and the 1st, 5th and 6th strings in the B♭ chord. You may not be able to manage this at first, but it will pay you to practise the use of the *Great Barré*, which will be very useful later on.

Notice that both the C7 and the B♭ contain the flattened B discussed above.

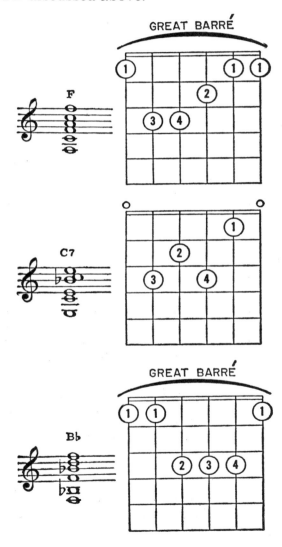

Now here is an exercise based on the arpeggios of these chords. This is a 12-bar blues progression, similar to the walking bass part given in the bass guitar chapter, but this time in a different key.

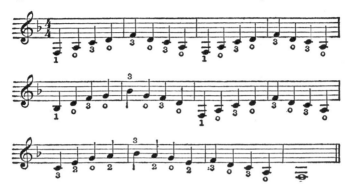

ALTERNATE PICKING

So far you should have been using all DOWN strokes of the plectrum. Now with the help of an elaboration on the exercise above I want you to try using UP strokes as well. In order to differentiate the two strokes, these signs are used:

⊓ **DOWN STROKE**

V **UP STROKE**

The purpose of this exercise is to begin the development of alternate picking – the use of alternate DOWN and UP strokes – a style favoured by most modern players. By striking the strings with the plectrum on both its downward and upward movement speed of execution can be considerably increased.

There should be no difference in tone between DOWN and UP strokes. For this reason the correct angle of the plectrum in relation to the strings becomes of great importance in the use of alternate picking.

Your UP strokes will no doubt be clumsy at first, but this fault can be overcome with practice, if you maintain the plectrum at a 90° angle to the strings. If, on the other hand, you have developed an incorrect habit of pushing the string downwards towards the body with the plectrum on the DOWN stroke, this will place your plectrum in the wrong position for its return on the UP stroke, and result in a thin 'pingy' tone.

Now try this exercise, using alternate picking, as indicated in the first two bars, throughout. You should produce an effect like the eight to a bar left hand of a boogie woogie piano player.

F chord

Chapter Twenty-One

THE KEY OF Bb

Bb is a favourite key in jazz playing. Possibly because, just as the keys of A and D are comfortable for the guitar, so is Bb an easy key for wind instruments such as trumpet and tenor saxophone.

The scale of Bb in the first position commences on

the first fret of the 5th string, like this:

As you will see from the scale above, there are two flattened notes in the Bb scale – Bb and Eb. The key signature of Bb is therefore:

And the scale, written more correctly is:

The exercise that follows is based on the scale of Bb. It should be practised first with all down strokes – then with alternate picking.

The three principal chords in the key of Bb are Bb, F7 and Eb.

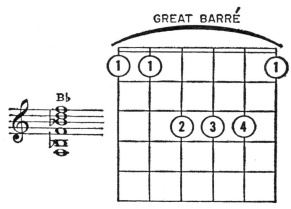

GREAT BARRÉ

135

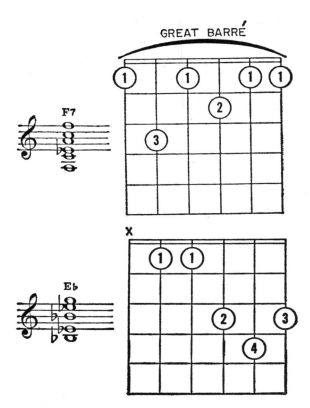

Here again we using the *Great Barré* in two chords. I realize that you may be having difficulty with this, but *do* stick with it because the *Great Barré* will become invaluable to you later on. As your first finger becomes stronger through practice you will gradually find yourself able to hold the *Barré* every time without rattles and with every note of the chord sounding clearly. Practise these chord shapes in B♭ carefully, getting the feel of changing from one to another.

I have written another piece in duo style for this chapter. A simple waltz with the melody in the bass (the notes with their tails pointing downwards.) The chords used are B♭, F7, E♭ and C7.

Notice particularly in this piece the use of ACCI-DENTALS. Accidentals are sharp or flat notes not contained in the original key signature, but indicated on the staff beside the note to which they apply. Thus we have the A♭ in Bar 16:

and the E natural in bar 21:

It should be noted that a sharp or a flat beside a note in this manner only applies for the space of the bar in which it appears. Say for instance in Example One below, the F sharp accidental on the second beat of the first bar applies equally to the F on the fourth beat of that bar. On the other hand, in Example Two, the F sharp in the first bar is automatically returned to F natural when F occurs in the second bar.

WELCOME WALTZ

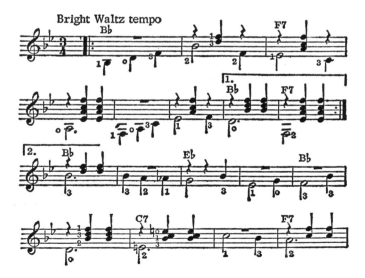

Chapter Twenty-Two

THE KEY OF E♭

All our scales and exercises so far have been in the first position – that is, with the first finger playing the notes on the first fret. This means that by now you should be fairly familiar with the notes of the first position – from F on the 6th string up to G on the 1st string.

Now, with the introduction of the key of E♭, we are going to move up into the Third Position. To start with, here are the principal chords in the key:

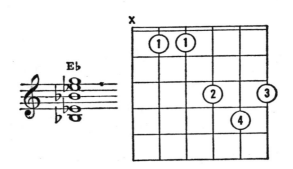

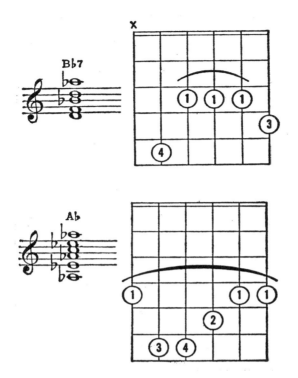

You should notice here that E♭ major is the same basic chord shape as the D you learned earlier on, but moved up a fret. Just as A♭ is the old F chord shape, moved up to the fourth fret. These are examples of MOVABLE CHORD SHAPES, which I shall be discussing more fully in Chapter Twenty-four.

Playing chords in these higher positions you will have to use increased left-hand pressure to make the notes sound clearly. Just how much difficulty you have is dependent on two main factors – the strength of your fingers, which should by now be feeling the benefit of constant practice; and the action of your guitar. Practise these chords carefully, until you are sure that you can get a full sound from each of them every time.

Now here is a scale of E♭ in the third position. The starting note is found by placing the fourth finger on the sixth fret of the 5th string.

A NOTE ON POSITION PLAYING

You may very well say at this point that you can play all the above notes in the first position, in fact, that you are able to play them in the first position with considerably more fluency. This may well be so, for a simple scale, but try the following, quite routine phrase, starting off in the first position. In the 3rd bar I have used a tied note – this indicates that the B♭ is picked only once, but carried on for one and a half beats.

How did it go? A bit of a shambles, wasn't it? Now here is the same phrase, but this time with the correct fingering indicated and played in the third position.

Played in this way the notes fall quite naturally under your fingers, don't they? Even allowing for the fact that you are not yet familiar with the notes this high on the fingerboard, after a bit of practice you should be able to play this phrase quite fluently, because your left hand doesn't have to jump up and down the fingerboard looking for the notes. This is briefly the purpose of position playing: To increase the facility of your left-hand fingering and improve your technical potential.

A lot of beginner soloists start out playing mainly on the 1st and 2nd strings, left-hand fingers leaping with varying accuracy up and down the fingerboard. Watch them, you'll see what I mean. Then watch a master of the instrument. You'll see that his left hand position changes much less frequently, because by using all six strings he has two whole octaves under his fingers *without changing position.* This is one of the reasons why so many of the uninitiated seem to think that solo guitar playing is easy. If you're doing it well, it *looks* easy.

I must admit quite freely that, as a self taught guitarist, the significance of position playing escaped me completely for a number of years. It was only when I found myself playing solo electric guitar with a quintet consisting of piano, bass, drums and accordion that I realized just how poor my technique was. Playing phrases in unison and harmony with an extremely fluent accordionist I was completely lost, stumbling clumsily through my parts. Thus it was a matter of sheer survival for me to find a better way of playing the seemingly 'impossible' phrases dreamed up by our arranger. Position playing is that better way. Without its help you can *never* become a first-class guitarist.

Now let's try an exercise in E♭, using the third position again. Watch the fingering indications carefully. Play the exercise slowly at first, maintain an even tempo. DOWN picking the first time – then ALTERNATE, as your left hand becomes used to the pattern it is making on the fingerboard.

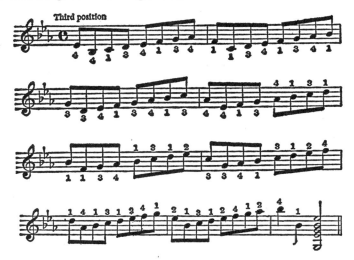

At the time I mentioned above, I spent a great deal of time practising single note piano studies and violin exercises, because there was not a great deal of this sort of material available for the guitar. This meant that I had to work out the fingering and positions as I went along – but today you are more fortunate, because there are a number of books of exercises on the market which give fingering and position indications.

Believe me, it is impossible to do too much of this sort of exercise. In addition to improving your technique, you will at the same time be gaining a greater fluency in your reading, and in associating the notes you read

with the actual fingerings on the guitar.
Here is another exercise in E♭.

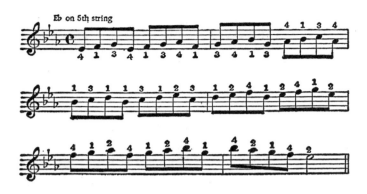

Chapter Twenty-Three

THE KEY OF A♭

The key in Ab has four flats in its key signature. It is particularly important when playing in a key with so many accidentals that you should remember to play them as such each time – *and not revert to playing naturals*. For this reason, considerable practice of exercises in such keys is advisable.

The basic A♭ falls most naturally in the third position, and the two octave scale can be played as fingered below, commencing with the second finger on the fourth fret of the 6th string.

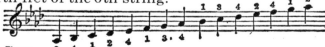

Practise this carefully, making sure that you are using the correct left-hand fingering. By cultivating correct fingering habits from the beginning, you should by now be well on the way towards developing that reflex we talked about earlier on.

Exercises of the type below are particularly useful in helping you to get the 'feel' of the key and its sound. If you memorize this kind of pattern you will find yourself automatically fingering the correct notes when reading a piece in A

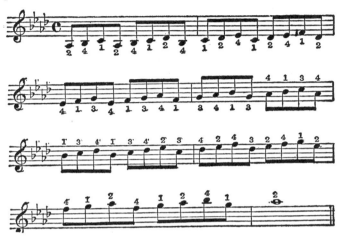

The principal chords in the key of A♭ are A♭, E♭7 and Db. You will notice that this time I have given you a different chord shape for A♭ from the one you have been using before. Practise this shape, and the others diligently, because we shall be using them again in the chapters that follow.

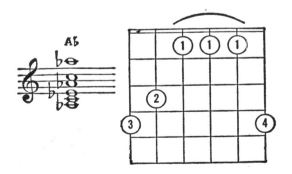

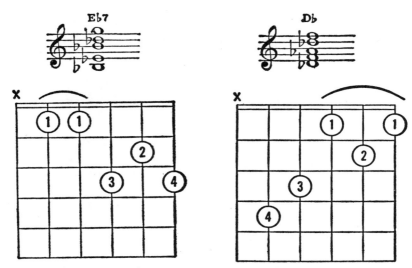

Now a solo in A♭. This is rather a different proposition to the old duo style, written in a style that mixes chords and single notes, and should prove a good reading exercise for you. It isn't really quite as difficult as it looks at first glance, because it is based for the most part on the arpeggios of basic chord shapes.

The first chord is C minor – played on the top three strings only, as shown in this window:

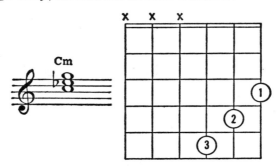

This chord should be held, while the B♭ note at the top is fingered by the fourth finger, making a C minor 7th.

The second chord, B minor, is exactly the same shape, but moved down a fret – and the A natural is added in the same way, with the fourth finger.

The chord in the second bar, B♭ minor is the same shape once again, and all the single notes in that bar are contained in its arpeggio. Then we have a bar of single notes, which fall easily under the fingers, followed by a full bar of an A♭ chord which is made by using a *Barré* on the 2nd, 3rd and 4th strings at the first fret.

MOOD PIECE

The fifth and sixth bars are arpeggios based on the same chords as those used in the first and second bars. Then in the seventh and eighth bars we have single notes again.

The middle section is written mainly in single notes, but I have put the names of the chords underneath wherever I feel that you may be able to use the full chord if your technique is good enough. After the middle eight we go back again to the theme established in the first section, using the same chord shapes.

I know that you're not going to be able to play MOOD PIECE at sight – I couldn't myself – but if you give it a bit of thought you should be able to work it out in time – and *constructive thought is worth far more than mere mechanical practice.*

Chapter Twenty-Four

MOVABLE CHORD SHAPES

Of all the advantages the guitar has to offer as an instrument, the concept of movable chord shapes is perhaps the most useful. It may be that the principle has already become self evident to you, through the practice you have done so far. If so, that's fine. But for those who haven't yet discovered them, here is an explanation of movable chord shapes.

You must have experienced – if you have been practising at all – the manner in which your fingers gradually become used to forming a chord shape on the fingerboard. Where at the beginning you had to make an individual effort to ensure the correct placing of each finger, you should now find that your left hand automatically forms the pattern of the chord shape you require. Take the common chord of F major, for instance:

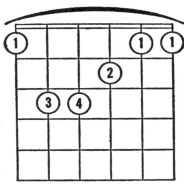

Now, without changing the relative positions of your left-hand fingers, slide the whole shape up one fret, so that the chord you are playing looks like this:

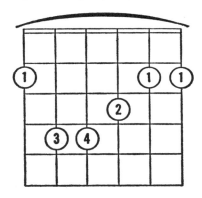

You are now, *without having changed the chord shape*, playing a chord of Gb major. Move the shape up another fret and the chord becomes G major ... another and it becomes Ab major. This process can be continued right up the fingerboard until you can go no further, because of the joint of the heel and body of the guitar.

For our purposes therefore, we can call this chord shape the basic F shape – named for the root note, which is to be found in this case on the 1st string – i.e. the note F. Thus it necessarily follows that wherever you play this chord shape on the fingerboard, the name of the major chord you are playing is the same as that of the note on the 1st string. On the fifth fret the chord becomes A major, on the eighth, C major, and so on . . . As an added bonus, you will find that the chord shape becomes easier to form as you go higher up the fingerboard and the frets become closer together.

I have used the basic F chord shape to illustrate, but in fact *any* chord shape which does not contain open strings is a movable chord shape. Clearly this is a tremendous step forward for you, because it means that with every chord shape you learn, you add a dozen chords to your repertoire. Or, at least, you *can* do so, if you know what the root note of the chord is, and where it is to be found on the fingerboard.

To enable you to take avantage of this, I have devoted the pages that follow to a summary of the more manageable movable chord shapes. In each case they are named for their lowest position on the fingerboard, and location of the root note is indicated.

Some of these chord shapes will be new to you, and some of them will merely be fuller versions of shapes you already know. *Learn them all sufficiently well to be able to place your left-hand fingers in position blindfold.*

Learn, too, the location of the root note in each case. Experiment with each shape, playing it in different positions - 1st, 5th, 9th, etc. - making sure that each time you are certain of the name of the chord you are playing. You will find the fingerboard chart a helpful guide in identifying the root notes at first - but don't use that crutch for longer than you're absolutely forced. A slower, but better way, is to work out the root note for yourself, *on the fingerboard itself.*

First we have three major shapes, all of them six-string chords. You will understand now my earlier insistence that you should practise the *Great Barré*, because its use is necessary in each case. If you still haven't mastered the *Barré*, you will have to content yourself with playing an abridged version; missing the 6th string in the case of the F and D♭, and the 5th and 6th in the B♭.

Here are the windows - play them, and *learn them.*

148

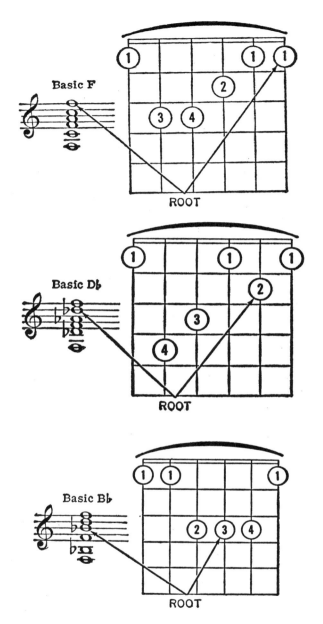

Basic F

Basic D♭

Basic B♭

Next in importance, the 7th chords. The F7 and B♭7 shapes are again six-string chords, using the *Barré*. The C7 is a four string *inside shape*, in which neither the 1st nor 6th strings should be sounded. This can be effected by either missing them with the stroke of the plectrum, or by deadening them with the side of one of your left-hand fingers. The method is a matter of personal taste and convenience. Some experimentation on your part is therefore advisable. The E♭ 7th shape is a five-string chord, using the top five strings only.

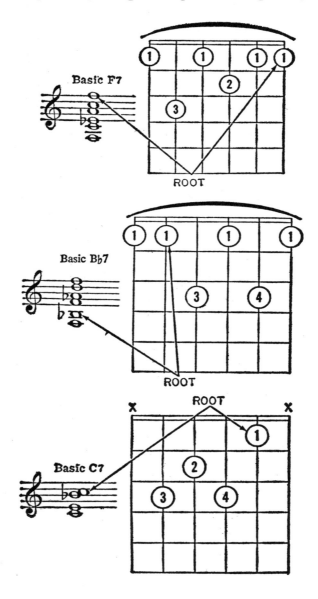

Basic F7

Basic B♭7

Basic C7

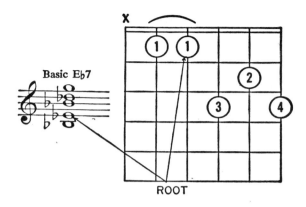

Basic Eb7

Next, because of its close relationship to the 7th chord - for which it can frequently be substituted - we come to the 9th chord. The basic B9 is a particularly useful and easy to play shape. Move it up a fret and you will see how closely it is related to the basic C7, *and* how easy it is to change from this shape to the basic F. The basic E9 is a four string chord only, missing as it does the 5th and 6th strings, but it has an interesting 'modern' sound. This shape is closely related to the basic F7.

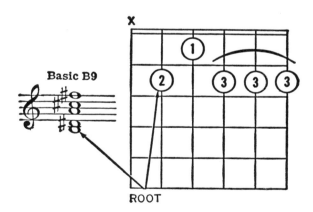

Basic B9

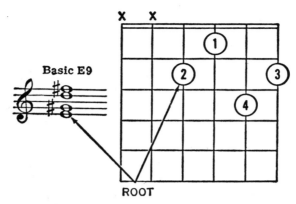

Basic E9

Next two six string minor chord shapes – full, sonorous sounding chords – and one four-string minor. The basic F minor and the basic B♭ minor both employ the *Barré*. The basic D minor, which is very closely related to the basic F major, requires the deadening, or missing of the 5th and 6th strings.

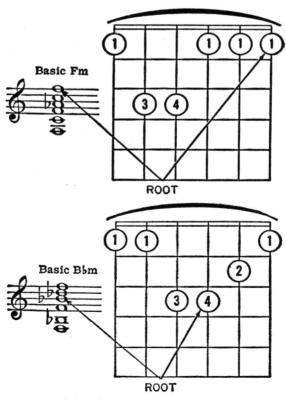

Basic Fm

Basic B♭m

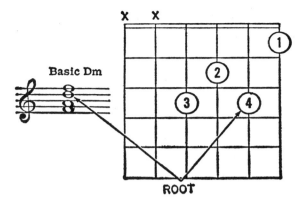

Basic Dm

The major 7th chord is closely related to the major; being a major chord with a major 7th interval added. That is, a note a semitone higher than the one used to form the ordinary (dominant) 7th. This chord is used a great deal in modern jazz – if you play it a few times the reason will become self evident. The two easiest forms are the basic Ab major 7 and the basic Eb major 7th.

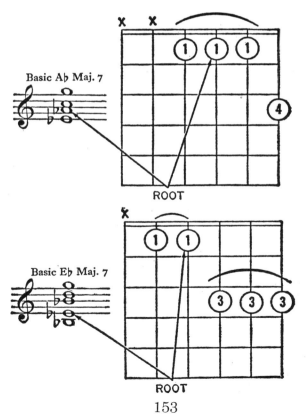

Basic Ab Maj. 7

Basic Eb Maj. 7

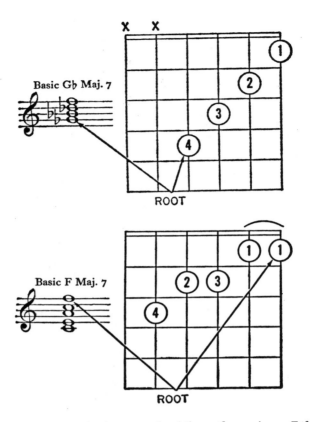

Basic G♭ Maj. 7

Basic F Maj. 7

Now we come to two curiosities, the minor 7th and the 6th chords. Curious, because as you will see from the guitarist's point of view they are equivalent to each other – WITH THE IMPORTANT PROVISO THAT THE ROOT IS TRANSFERRED.

Here are the basic A minor 7th and the basic C 6th, side by side. As you will see, they are identical.

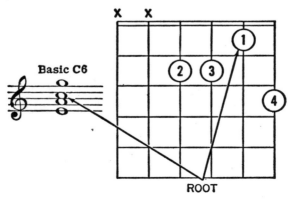

Basic C6

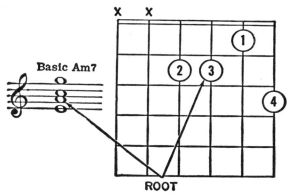

You may remember we learned earlier that A minor is the relative minor key to C major. A is also the 6th note of the C scale, upon which the C6 chord is based. A min 7th, being based on the A minor scale, has G as its seventh degree. Thus we have these chords with interchangeable names.

Here are two more basic minor 7th shapes – with their 6th equivalents side by side:

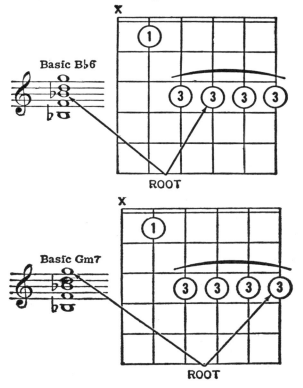

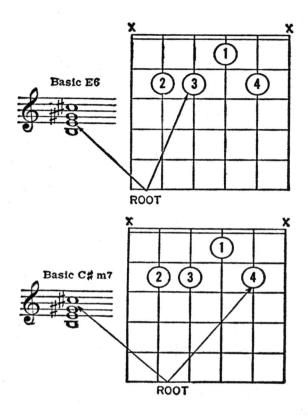

The diminisheds, if you remember our earlier explanation, should present very little difficulty. The main thing to remember is that a diminished chord can be named for any one of the notes it contains – so there is always a diminished readily available for you whatever position you are playing in.

The first shape below is the original four-string version which you have learned already; the second is a rather more grand five-string job, which can in fact be made into a six-string chord by extending your first finger across in a *Barré* to the 6th string.

156

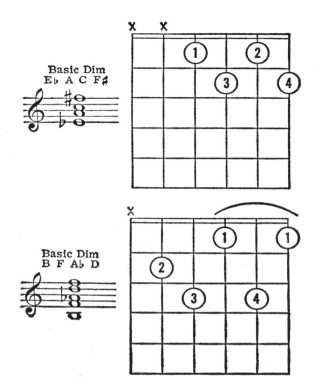

Basic Dim
Eb A C F#

Basic Dim
B F Ab D

In this chapter you have all the information on chords that you will need for some time to come. Now it is up to you to practise these basic shapes and learn to identify them in any position on the fingerboard.

And don't stop practising them until you can pass the blindfold test every time . . .

Chapter Twenty-Five
WHAT NOW?

When we started out at Chapter One I was careful not to make any false promises. You should have come a long way since then. Just how far depends on how much work you've put in. Work! What am I talking about? If you've got to this point, playing the guitar must be a pleasure for you, and that's how it should be. There's a lot more to learn. There always will be. That's one of the things that makes the guitar so interesting and rewarding. The study that you can just about struggle through today will turn into a flowing, fully realized piece of music within a week or two, if you keep on practising it and give the magical processes of memory, both muscular and intellectual, time to play their part. Believe me, it works! I've proved it to myself, and so can you.

Our little journey in this book has been only a step along the road, so don't stop now. There are people and books to help you to progress just as far as you want to go. By now you should have some idea of both your potential ability and the nature of your goal; so let's take a brief look at some aids to further study.

If you want to play plectrum guitar really well, your next step could be to work your way through the Ivor Mairants Complete Guitar Tutor, published by Francis, Day and Hunter Ltd. When you've mastered this book your playing will be of – I was going to say 'professional' standard, but there are many so-called professionals today who couldn't get through the first twenty-five pages. If you have cultivated the right practice habits with the aid of GUITAR then you should be able to tackle Ivor's excellent method. But once again let me warn you: Don't expect any golden key. You'll only get what you put into it.

If you're technically minded and into jazz improvisation I would suggest that you then take a look at the books written by Ted Greene, particularly CHORD CHEMISTRY and JAZZ GUITAR. SINGLE NOTE SOLOING. I've never met Ted Greene, because he lives on the other side of the Atlantic, but he must be a man of incredible dedication and intellect. These books are like nothing you'll ever encounter elsewhere in their encyclopedic approach to chords and arpeggios and will provide you with sufficient material for years of study. Don't, whatever you do, try to swallow them whole, or you're bound to end up with mental indigestion.

If you're into jazz chordal soloing you might also like to have a look at JOE PASS CHORD SOLOS, which contains transcriptions of the master's solos on a number of well known jazz standards such as MISTY and DAYS OF WINE AND ROSES. They're not easy to play of course, but they will give you a greater insight into the way the mind of this great player works. The same applies to JOE PASS GUITAR CHORDS, which is a book of chord shapes intended to help you develop your knowledge of and feeling for Fingerboard Harmony.

If you're into rock you will want to take a look at ORIGINAL JIMI HENDRIX by Steve Tarshis and Larry Coryell's record and music set IMPROVISATION FROM ROCK TO JAZZ.

Moving on to Spanish Guitar probably the best basic training you are likely to get is to study the works of Frederick M. Noad: SOLO GUITAR PLAYING – Books 1 and 2. As with the Ivor Mairants book for Plectrum guitar, if you have worked sincerely through these books you will be well on your way to becoming a good player.

Any list I might make of pieces in the Classical repertoire would be incomplete, so I won't even attempt it. You will no doubt have your own favourites and most of these are readily available from specialist music houses like those mentioned at the end of this section. I would, however, like to point you in the direction of several interesting byroads open to the player of the Finger Style guitar.

Howard Morgen has written two books under the heading of FINGERSTYLE JAZZ AND POPULAR GUITAR. The first is called PREPARATIONS and is intended for the comparative beginner, the second: CONCEPTS rather more advanced. I have found CONCEPTS particularly useful in helping develop my own individual brand of Spanish Guitar jazz. This book will really move you along the road to playing 'Lap Piano', a style of self-contained solo guitar which really makes use of all the possibilities of the instrument.

There are a number of FLAMENCO methods on the market, some of which I have not had the opportunity of studying, but for clear explanations and good musical examples I would still recommend the old maestro himself, Ivor Mairants, whose book FLAMENCO GUITAR provides a thorough grounding in the genre.

I mentioned BRAZILIAN MUSIC in an earlier chapter, as a whole new world of fascinating rhythms and melodies. Jack Marshall's BOSSA NOVA Guitar Arrangements would serve as a good, not too difficult introduction to this field. From there you might go on to THE BRAZILIAN MASTERS by Brian Hodel and after that into the Baden Powell collections. There's a tremendous amount of stuff written for this type of guitar playing, so you won't be short of material once you're into it.

I should say a word too about Finger Picking – the kind of Folk/Blues guitar this is played on either steel strings or nylon. Stefan Grossman has made something of a speciality of writing books on this style and you might like to start off by trying his FINGER PICKING SOLOS or CONTEMPORARY RAGTIME GUITAR.

The above is of necessity only a small selection of the books available on the different styles of guitar playing. I have copies of them all and many more, but these have been collected over many years of guitar playing and I don't suggest that you rush out and buy the lot straight away, even if you could afford it. Your changing interests will dictate which ones have priority for you personally.

You will be very fortunate if you have a local music store which stocks all titles you want, but you should at least give them a try first. Failing that, you will almost certainly get what you want from either: Ivor Mairants Musicentre, 56 Rathbone Place, LONDON, W1; The Guitar Shop, 3 Bimport, SHAFTESBURY, Dorset or the ASHLEY MARK PUBLISHING COMPANY, Saltmeadows Road, GATESHEAD, NE8 3AJ, who publish a very comprehensive Guitar Music Catalogue which includes most of the books mentioned above.

MAGAZINES

There are at the present time three good magazines devoted to the guitar: CLASSICAL GUITAR published by the Ashley Mark Publishing Co, whose address is given above. GUITAR published by Musical New Services at Bimport, SHAFTESBURY, Dorset and the US magazine GUITAR PLAYER which you can often pick up in shops that specialize in guitars. They are all good value, and which one you prefer will depend to a great extent on your own particular field of interest. If you're an addict like me you'll probably end up with all three!

TEACHERS

Books like this will help you along if you're struggling on your own, but nothing can take the place of a good teacher, someone with whom you can discuss your playing problems on a personal basis. He will be able to listen to your playing and help guide you in conquering your personal weaknesses. The magazines usually run a directory of teachers, so you can easily find out who to contact in your own area.

GUITAR SOCIETIES

These can be very rewarding, especially for a beginner, because they will give you the opportunity of meeting other players on a regular basis. You may get into duet playing, which can be fun. Or you may get over the psychological hurdle of your first 'public' performance on one of the members 'do it yourself' nights. The magazines will tell you if there is a society near you, so if there is, why not give it a try?

SCHOOLS & SEMINARS

There are a number of Summer Schools and Weekend Seminars devoted to various types of playing. Once again these will give you an opportunity to meet other players, and I believe this to be very important. Nothing is more stimulating than to spend a number of days and nights in the company of a group of fellow guitarists, some of whom may be far ahead of you in development, others way behind.

Guitar playing is not competitive, but when you meet somebody personally who plays very well it can set ambition buzzing in your own mind, along the lines of: 'If he/ she can play like that, why not me? And what am I going to do about it?' Whatever happens, take my word for it from personal experience, you will come away with your batteries fully charged and a determination to improve your playing.

A word of caution. This type of course is not usually aimed at the absolute beginner, so try and get some basic grounding under your belt before you go. That's not to say that you won't be welcome whatever your standard. Guitar players are not snobs and even if your playing is terrible you're bound to find someone who will be only too pleased to help.

On a personal note could I say that if you are really into jazz you'll be missing the chance of a lifetime if you don't find some way of attending one of Barney Kessel's EFFECTIVE GUITARIST Seminars, which are usually held in late October or early November at Newcastle on Tyne.

You will find details of the various seminars and courses in the magazines mentioned above if you want to know more.

Finally, I can only hope that guitar playing brings you as much pleasure as it has given me over the years. I'll leave the last word to the lady who has listened uncomplainingly to my practice for a very long time:

GEORGINA